creative ESSENTIALS

LUCY V. HAY

WRITING AND SELLING
DRAMA SCREENPLAYS

creative ESSENTIALS

First published in 2014 by Kamera Books,
an imprint of Oldcastle Books,
PO Box 394, Harpenden, Herts, AL5 1XJ
www.kamerabooks.com

Copyright © Lucy V. Hay 2014
Series Editor: Hannah Patterson
Editor: Anne Hudson

A CIP catalogue record for this book is available from the British Library.

978-1-84344-412-1   (Print)
978-1-84344-413-8   (epub)
978-1-84344-414-5   (kindle)
978-1-84344-415-2   (pdf)

4 6 8 10 9 7 5

Typeset by Elsa Mathern in Franklin Gothic 9 pt
Printed in Great Britain by 4edge Limited, Essex

*For all the writers and filmmakers who were so generous
with their time and insights in making this book possible,
plus the Bang2writers who keep me on my toes!*

CONTENTS

Preface 9

WHAT DRAMA IS NOT (AND BEYOND) 13

WRITING VERSUS SELLING 22

TRUTH AND DARE 42

THE PSYCHE AND CONFLICT 56

COMMON WRITER AND DRAMA MISTAKES 71

KNOW YOUR DRAMA NICHE 88

BEATING THE ODDS 109

TRUE BLUE 130

NO ONE SIZE FITS ALL 140

WHATEVER IT TAKES 165

WRITING AND SELLING YOUR OWN SPEC DRAMA SCREENPLAY ... 179

ADDENDUM 185

Resources 190
Index 204

PREFACE

Bang2write and its accompanying social network is often cited online by others as being for those interested in genre writing, and certainly my articles on the differences between horror and thriller remain some of the most oft-hit on the site. But I've always had an affinity for drama. Though I've always enjoyed thrillers and horror, plus blockbusters and their ilk (and no doubt always will), it was actually drama that lit a fire under me in terms of storytelling. I did a media course as a teenager and one of our first assignments was to do a review of a non-Hollywood film (no doubt our lecturer's attempt to challenge media imperialism... for me, it worked!). Back then there was no Netflix, Amazon Prime or YouTube; there was barely DVD. So I went to the local video store and my mate Dylan recommended *Once Were Warriors* (1994), a New Zealand drama about a family descended from Maoris whose story involved domestic violence, sexual abuse and bereavement after a suicide. I'll be honest and say that, back then, as a young white girl in rural Devon, I was completely unaware of Maori people (never mind the fact that they're often treated as outcasts despite being indigenous to New Zealand), so it was a huge eye-opener for me. Though I didn't know the word 'disenfranchisement' then, I was struck by the themes of injustice and loss in the film, and it was like a million light bulbs went on in my head. For the first time, I realised movies could be challenging, as well as entertaining.

Fast-forward a few years and I was on my first work placement, as a script reader for a literary agent. The UK is known for hard-hitting, realistic, gritty drama and it reached a particular high point in the 1990s, so it's not really surprising that, in the early noughties, there was a plethora of very worthy, low-budget drama screenplays in the spec pile (most of them feature-length, inspired by the likes of Loach, Leigh and Russell). Though this appears to have dropped off in recent years (especially in favour of science fiction and fantasy TV pilot screenplays for returning series, interestingly), I still read a lot of spec drama screenplays. I'd wager at least 30 per cent of Bang2write's general submissions pile is drama, whether short film, feature, TV pilot or web series, as it seems spec screenwriters and filmmakers love to try to put 'real life' under the microscope. And why not? We all want to make sense of the world around us.

Writers also frequently target low-budget drama as a handy 'foot in the door' to the industry. However, whilst they're right that it gives their screenplays a greater likelihood of being produced (especially short-film drama screenplays), there appears to be a fundamental misunderstanding amongst many about just what a well-conceived drama screenplay entails. This may be due not only to the story or characters they choose, but also to arena, storytelling devices (like flashback), and dialogue. In the course of this book, then, I will break down what drama means to me as an avid consumer of such produced content and reader of (often 'misfiring'!) drama screenplays. I will also look at the common mistakes of spec dramas, especially with reference to character, storytelling and structure. In addition, I will look at a number of produced dramas of varying types, including (but not limited to) short films, adaptations and star-led vehicles. I will also look at the concept of theme and message, as well as target audience and budget. Last of all, since I focused on filmmaking resources in my previous screenwriting book (and many will obviously cross over), I have created a very different resource for the back of this book. I hope you like it.

Though produced dramas may win the most awards and kudos from critics, you're unlikely to sell a drama feature screenplay as easily as you might a genre script, at least in the current marketplace. Breaking down the nuts and bolts of what differentiates drama from genre film, *Writing and Selling Drama Screenplays* will guide you to an understanding of how the best drama feature screenplays are NOT about abject misery or using stereotypical depictions of socio-ethnic groups to get their messages across. It will also open the lid on the struggles of screenwriters and producers in getting their own projects off the ground. As usual, there will be spoilers in abundance, including detailed case studies of produced dramas (and one currently unproduced), which will give you the truth – and nothing but the truth – on just how much of a labour of love it is to get your drama screenplay made and out there, in front of an audience. Think you're wo/man enough to do it?

Lucy V, September 2014

WHAT DRAMA IS NOT (AND BEYOND)

DRAMA VERSUS GENRE

Many writers confess to being unsure what 'drama' really is. If you look online, you will often see the label used interchangeably with 'genre'. On IMDb, most films appear to be tagged 'drama' and many writers will argue that drama is a genre in its own right. But forget how you personally feel about drama and what it is. What's key here is how the *Industry* perceives genre and drama:

'Genre' – think BIG stories; event-driven with high (typically life-or-death) stakes; stylised storytelling; often highly commercial with large audience appeal

and

'Drama' – think SMALL stories; individuals; relationships; private moments; tragedies; personal; emotional; typically niche audience

Or in other words:

- **GENRE:** horror, thriller, comedy, and all their subtypes and mash-ups; mostly star-led; so-called 'plausibility' secondary; epic arenas; special effects; explosions; often large casts of secondary and peripheral characters; often mammoth productions with large crews; very frequently high-budget, but also micro-budget productions with minimal characters and locations – though they will generally need to be large in scope, aka 'high-concept'.

- **DRAMA**: everything else! Character actors, rather than big stars (though there may be a few); plausibility a high priority; some larger than average arenas, but mostly smaller; generally minimal locations and characters; often small productions with small crews and low budgets (relatively speaking, even when seemingly 'high-budget').

Of course, no definitive checklist exists for any story (and nor should it). What's more, drama can basically be about pretty much anything, so it's perhaps more advantageous at this juncture to pin down what drama definitely is NOT, namely:

- *'Big' in scope.* Stories are predominantly personal affairs, and even those dramas that unfold across a broad canvas, both geographically and temporally, are still 'smaller' than a large-budget action-adventure, thriller or horror that does the same. What's more, even a produced drama with a budget of millions will still clock in at far less than its nearest genre counterpart.

- *Event-led.* As drama stories are largely personal, the target audience for this kind of produced content is signing up to see the world view of a set of characters, namely their responses to the situations in the story and the effect on them and others. Resolution comes NOT from solving a problem or resolving an issue so much as 'coming to terms' with it. This means a writer has to render a metaphorical concept physically as image, which is why dramas are so damn difficult to write!

Now let's look at some produced dramas and consider what 'makes' them and why they may be popular.

POPULAR PRODUCED DRAMAS ON IMDb

As mentioned already, just about every produced film or show listed on IMDb is tagged 'drama' (which can add to scribes' confusion). On this basis, then, I decided to do an advanced search for a 'typical' type of drama. I chose the word 'biopic', a biographical drama based on the life of someone who (usually!) really existed, either famous or not so famous, but generally noted for doing something remarkable and/or infamous in so-called 'real life.' Now, allowing for the (general) US bias of IMDb (meaning these are predominantly star-led dramas), and excluding television, TV movies and documentary, these were the top 20 most popular biopic searches on IMDb at the time of writing:

1. *Goodfellas* (1990). IMDb Rating: 8.8. The story of Henry Hill, who worked his way up the mob hierarchy of 1950s Brooklyn. Adaptation (book).

2. *A Beautiful Mind* (2001). IMDb Rating: 8.2. The story of brilliant mathematician and Nobel Prize winner John Nash. Adaptation (book).

3. *Alexander* (2004). IMDb Rating: 5.5. Biopic of the ancient king of Macedonia, who conquered most of the known world.

4. *The King's Speech* (2010). IMDb Rating: 8.1. The story of King George VI, who had a stutter and needed speech therapy on taking the British throne.

5. *J Edgar* (2011). IMDb Rating: 6.6. Powerful head of the FBI for 50 years, J Edgar Hoover looks back on his professional and personal life.

6. *50 to 1* (2014). IMDb Rating: 7.9. Story of the 2009 Kentucky Derby winner, 'Mine That Bird', who triumphed against 50 to 1 odds.

7. *Ed Wood* (1994). IMDb Rating: 7.9. Story of the legendary eccentric director, claimed to have made the worst movies ever. Adaptation (book).

8. *The Iron Lady* (2011). IMDb Rating: 6.4. Biography of UK's first and only female prime minister. Female screenwriter AND director.

9. *Man on the Moon* (1999). IMDb Rating: 7.5. The life and times of eccentric comedian, entertainer and star of Taxi, Andy Kaufman.

10. *Serpico* (1973). IMDb Rating: 7.8. The true story of an honest New York cop turned whistleblower on force corruption. Adaptation (book).

11. *The Express* (2008). IMDb Rating: 7.3. Drama based on the life of college football hero Ernie Davis, the first African-American to win the Heisman Trophy. Adaptation (book).

12. *Stand and Deliver* (1988). IMDb Rating: 7.4. The story of Jaime Escalante, a high-school teacher who successfully inspired his dropout-prone students to learn calculus.

13. *Sweet and Lowdown* (1999). IMDb Rating: 7.3. In the 1930s, fictional jazz guitarist Emmet Ray idolises Django Reinhardt, faces gangsters and falls in love with a mute.

14. *Bird* (1988). IMDb Rating: 7.2. The troubled life and career of the jazz musician, Charlie 'Bird' Parker.

15. *The Pride of the Yankees* (1942). IMDb Rating: 7.8. The story of the life and career of the famed baseball player, Lou Gehrig, whose name is still synonymous with motor neurone disease in the USA.

16. *The Babe* (1992). IMDb Rating: 5.8. Biography of the baseball player Babe Ruth, especially his relationships with others off the field.

17. *Dark Victory* (1939). IMDb Rating: 7.6. Cancer story about a young society 'it girl' diagnosed with an inoperable brain tumour. Adaptation (play).

18. *Till the Clouds Roll By* (1946). IMDb Rating: 6.5. Biopic of the Broadway pioneer Jerome Kern, featuring many of his most famous songs.

19. *Modigliani* (2004). IMDb Rating: 7.4. The story of painter and sculptor Modigliani's bitter rivalry with Pablo Picasso, and his tragic romance with Jeanne Hebuterne.

20. *Knute Rockne All American* (1940). IMDb Rating: 6.9. The story of legendary Notre Dame football player and coach Knute Rockne.

What I find interesting about this list:

- **The age of the movies.** I was expecting to see mostly new movies turn up as the most searched for with the keyword 'biopic' and was really surprised to see only one film – *50 to 1* – coming up from 2014, not to mention a movie nearly 25 years old in the top spot, i.e. *Goodfellas*. Of course, Scorsese is an icon, but he has also made several dramas since *Goodfellas*, so it's really interesting that this was his most popular on the day of my search. I was also intrigued by the number of produced biopics from the thirties and forties, not to mention the complete lack of ones from the fifties and sixties, with only one turning up from the 1970s.

- **The subject matter of the biopics.** I was unsurprised to see kings, politicians, FBI head honchos and the like dominating the list: target audiences are always interested in powerful people and what they're like 'behind closed doors'. Similarly, I figured I would see a number of famous people, like comedians, film directors or sports stars. What did surprise me, however, was the number of dramas about musicians and artists and the relative lack of stories about illness, particularly cancer stories (just one in the top 20 in *Dark Victory*), especially since cancer stories are so prevalent in the spec pile. I was also very surprised at the lack of crime stories here, since crime is also a popular subject matter for spec drama screenplays, especially British ones.

- *Adaptation.* All the films are adaptations in the sense that the stories are about real people (if not the protagonists, then the secondary characters, though this was difficult to check in the case of some of the older movies). However, a large number of them aren't adapted directly from books (fiction or non-fiction) or plays, which I found surprising.

- *Age, race and gender.* As ever, the majority of protagonists are white males, though some are older than the 25–40-year-old protagonists generally expected in genre films. There are some female protagonists, and if people of colour figure in the list it's usually as sports players or, in one case, a teacher. Several of the true stories here talk about either the 'troubled' or 'eccentric' lives of the main characters. Last of all, and somewhat inevitably, the vast majority of screenwriters and directors are male – though, intriguingly, *50 to 1*, which deals with the traditionally 'masculine' sport of horse racing, has not one but two female co-screenwriters.

Whilst not a magic bullet or even a recommended way of making concrete market decisions, IMDb can perform a useful function for both writers and filmmakers in showing various trends and flagging up the potential interests of audiences. In my experience, many writers use IMDb in a very sporadic way: they may check titles or dream-cast stars in lead roles in their screenplays. Yet knowing what has gone before (if anything) in the arena of your chosen drama idea is crucial research for the spec screenwriter, as is knowing how previous works have approached the subject matter, so you can differentiate yours (so it's not a story that has essentially 'already been told'). Now, obviously, writers should not write solely for the market; that's madness, especially when a spec drama screenplay SHOULD be both personal and passionate in terms of subject, story and characters. However, doing one's research can help inform one's approach to a story – or even stop a writer from wasting his or her time writing a complete duffer! What's not to like?

CASE STUDIES IN THIS BOOK

The word most commonly seen in relation to 'drama' online is 'depressing', but I will venture to argue later in this book that this is where many writers' misunderstanding of drama screenplays begins. For now, I posit the notion once more: 'real' drama is NOT about abject misery, dying and/or losing all hope. Instead, I believe drama is about STRUGGLE. No human being leads a charmed life; we will ALL struggle in the course of our lives, so it's not difficult to see what is appealing about watching characters doing the same on screen.

The UK has a rich history of drama in terms of produced content. Since our little island frequently wins both international recognition and awards for its drama, I have attempted to ensure the films chosen for the case studies in this book are predominantly British. I have also included 'non-typical' characters and makers in terms of age, race and gender, including (but not limited to) female directors where possible. Here are my loglines for the projects I will discuss:

The Short Film

Cancer Hair (2014). A young woman, in remission from cancer and wearing a wig, attempts to go on a blind date but comes unstuck.

The True Story

Saving Mr Banks (2013). All about the battle of wills between Walt Disney and author PL Travers over the rights and adaptation of the classic novel, Mary Poppins.

The Enlightenment Story

Dear Frankie (2004). A single mother writes letters to her son, pretending they are from his dad who she says is away at sea.

When 'his' ship docks in their town, however, she is forced to hire a stranger to play the role of Frankie's father.

The Morality Tale

Kidulthood (2006). After the suicide of a fellow student, a group of teenagers get the day off school, which ends with violence, mayhem and even murder.

The Portmanteau Story

Night People (2005). Told over the course of one night, a selection of people must make a decision that changes their lives forever.

The Coming Out/Coming of Age Story

Beautiful Thing (1996). When a young teenage boy's abused neighbour comes to stay, the two lads experience new feelings and realise why neither of them has ever quite fitted in with their peers.

The Responsibility Story

Hours (2013). Newly widowed, a lone father has to keep his premature daughter alive in an incubator in a hospital that has no power and limited supplies due to Hurricane Katrina.

The Family Drama

Rocketboy (Unproduced). An old man recounts his childhood building rockets with his grandfather, detailing how he fell in love along the way.

As you will see, I have also tried to make sure that most of the case studies (and other produced dramas I mention) are relatively recent. The industry is constantly in a state of flux, plus many column inches online and in other books have been dedicated to 'classic' dramas (accounting in part perhaps for why screenwriters end up recycling 'old' material or tropes and writing 'movies of movies', rather than letting personal experience drive their stories). Last of all, I also felt all the works here were made well and were interesting! But even if you do not care for the individual movies or their subject matters, I still recommend you watch the works cited here (again, if necessary), to gain the most insight possible from this book and avoid the usual traps so many drama spec screenplays fall into.

YOUR OWN DRAMA SCREENPLAYS

It should be noted that, whilst I have concentrated on feature-length drama screenplays in the writing of this book, this is because there is, in my opinion, a significant dearth in the spec pile of authentic drama features with non-clichéd characters and non-samey stories! I would venture that drama feature screenplays achievable on budgets of £500,000 (or lower) offer significant opportunities for writers to attract producers and filmmakers. However, an individual writer's format preference will obviously be their own, and the key element of drama – an emotional, well-conceived, character-led story with light AND shade – lends itself to short film, TV pilots and web series just as easily. So whatever route you choose to go for, keep in mind the 'essence' of good drama from the case studies I've chosen, rather than believing that movies are somehow different, because they're not. And, whatever you do, NEVER attempt to tick boxes – miserable character (CHECK!); miserable life (CHECK!); miserable story world (CHECK!) – in the hope of satisfying a producer or filmmaker out there who wants some dire, depressing screenplay, because they DON'T!

But what *do* they want? Let's find out...

WRITING VERSUS SELLING

WRITING DRAMA SCREENPLAYS

'Low-budget drama' is a phrase that may invoke trepidation in any script reader, producer, exec, agent or filmmaker. Why? Because, too often, writers will mean the following when pitching their drama:

'A miserable character leads a miserable life THEN DIES (or worse)!'

The story will frequently include extremely two-dimensional, clichéd characters and other storytelling elements (poor people living in sinkhole estates is the favourite). Never underestimate how many writers are churning out the same-old, same-old, with little chance for innovation. Yet, in my experience, writers are extremely reluctant to confront this about their own drama screenplays. Whilst, obviously, no one wants to accept they've conceived a stereotypical story with rubbish characters, the level of self-delusion some writers indulge in can be total. 'But if I've written it, then it's my unique voice! Surely that will carry my story through?' they might insist.

No! A million times, no. These are the facts: not only will it take not writing 'the usual' to get you noticed; drama screenplays have to be about SO MUCH MORE than concrete shitholes, teenage mums and drug dealer boyfriends. You need only look around your local DVD store (if it still exists!) to confirm this. There's simply no excuse for dropping storytelling cliché clangers. But that's the bad news.

The good news is, it's the same as writing any other kind of spec screenplay. YOU'RE the writer! You can write about whatever you want, just so long as it's within the parameters of a great story that's fresh and original, with characters who feel real, confronting issues, scenarios and problems that seem authentic and relevant to your target audience. And the second bit of good news? You're not the first writer and/or filmmaker to tread this ground, hence the drama case studies here! I have broken down what we can learn from each one into two parts – 'write tips' and 'selling points' – at the end of each case study.

SELLING DRAMA SCREENPLAYS

This is the thing: you probably won't get rich off a produced drama screenplay (well, you probably won't get rich off any one screenplay, to be quite honest, especially outside LA). But whilst it is at least possible to get paid actual money for the most marketable, high-concept, spec genre screenplays (especially comedy, horror and thriller), there is a strong likelihood you will be paying your OWN money out to get your drama screenplay produced. Yes, you read that right. The sad fact of the matter is, produced drama content is frequently a 'labour of love' for all involved: writer, producer, director... sometimes even the named talent starring in them! Michelle Williams was a huge star at a young age in the nineties thanks to teen-angst TV drama series *Dawson's Creek*. Even before her Oscar nominations for *Brokeback Mountain* (2005) and *My Week with Marilyn* (2011), she 'just knew' she had to star in *Blue Valentine* (2010), no matter what. '[It] took years to get off the ground and I was able to stick with it,' she later told Lynn Hirschberg in *W* magazine. 'I first read the script when I was 21, 22, and it became my reason for being for the longest time. When I ran into Ryan [Gosling], he said, "What about that movie?" I was surprised; I thought *Blue Valentine* existed only in my head. Until he said that, I was worried it wasn't quite as good as I had thought. He validated my reaction.'

On this basis, then, I will not be talking in this book about selling drama screenplays the 'traditional' way because the sad reality is, if it's still hard for filmmakers to get their drama productions made with the likes of Michelle Williams and Ryan Gosling attached, then the rest of us mere mortals have to think even MORE creatively to get ours made, sold and out there! What's more, Williams hits the nail on the head when it comes to getting people – producers, filmmakers, investors, even distributors – on board our own drama screenplays when she says, 'I was worried [*Blue Valentine*] wasn't quite as good as I thought.'

It's really important to remember that the key strength of a well-written drama screenplay is the personal nature of its story, but it can also be its main weakness. Genre screenplays with strong hooks may immediately speak to the fears or desires of mass audiences and thus 'sell them off the page' in just a sentence or two, the very definition of 'high-concept'. In comparison, it's much harder to do the same for even the best-written drama screenplays. Dramas by their very nature are those kinds of stories about the minutiae of life, so reducing them to grass-roots level in the same way as a genre screenplay may make those stories seem puzzling to others or, at worst, even dull. With just a logline, and without the opportunity to walk industry pros through the characters, their world views and one's own motivation for wanting to write and make such a screenplay (not to mention what the audience might get out of it), it's extremely unlikely that a writer will be able to interest others in their idea. But my purpose here is NOT to depress writers and say it can't be done, because it obviously can! But you DO have to make it happen for yourself and for your work, arguably even more than you would with a genre screenplay.

So forget about the traditional channels and methods. Instead, you will need to work on a number of things, all of them obvious, the first being the story and characters. Whilst ALL spec screenplays must stand head and shoulders above the rest in terms of story and characters (not to mention compete with producers' own ideas for stories!), at a grass-roots level it's arguably 'concept' that's key to a sale when genre writing. As unpopular as it is to admit it, many genre movies with underwritten stories and paper-thin characters DO get made, and audiences often flock to see them. This is not because audiences are stupid, or even easily pleased, but because they are attracted to different produced content for different reasons. It is well known that a person (especially one who is not a writer or involved in the industry) may watch a movie with an underdeveloped story and/or characters because s/he is primarily interested in the spectacle of it, especially when it comes to Hollywood blockbusters. People may watch a movie for curiosity or nostalgia's sake, too: this is why remakes, reboots and movies about children's toys are also popular. When it comes to low-budget genre screenplays, indie filmmakers obviously don't have the luxury of being able to realise their vision on as grand a scale. However, they CAN still indulge their audiences' desire for spectacle in ways that do not cost much money. The most obvious example is the horror genre, particularly so-called 'torture porn'. Audiences who enjoy the extreme suffering of people on screen often don't care whether those characters are well developed; the audience just wants to see gore. Other low-budget horrors and some thrillers, especially the supernatural kind, may create similar levels of fear via suspense, making their audiences jump via techniques commonly used in found footage-type stories.

In comparison, then, a drama screenplay – whether it's ten thousand or ten million pounds' worth (or even more!) – is ALWAYS a much harder sell from the offset, which is why its characters and story must be absolutely watertight. When there are more spec screenplays and projects in development than could EVER be made, with millions more being written every single day, your characters and story must ROCK to be even in with a chance of catching someone's attention. This is because just about everyone in the industry, big or small, has a 'great idea' for a drama, a passion project, something they want to do even though everyone else might tell them they're CRAZY. So, that's the first hurdle writers have to jump: they have to persuade others they should make THEIR passion project, instead of their own. The second hurdle: is YOUR project as 'good' as you think it is? Remember Michelle Williams and Ryan Gosling. They might have loved *Blue Valentine*, but until it was actually made, no one on that production – not even two child actors who had grown up to be big Hollywood stars – could have known whether audiences would respond to it. Whilst it's certainly true that this a gamble where ALL films are concerned, genre pieces do have a kind of framework to work within, based on convention and audience expectation. Chances are that 'if an audience liked X, then they'll probably like Y', especially if it's in the same kind of ballpark, by the same people. This is why so many movie posters proclaim, 'From the director of...' or 'From the producers who brought you...' Dramas, on the other hand, have no such framework. Remember that they can be about anything, using any storytelling devices and methods they want, with characters of any kind. As a result, produced dramas can be the ultimate crapshoot: what looks good on paper can be disastrous financially, or vice versa!

Luckily for everyone involved in *Blue Valentine*, audiences responded wildly, with the movie winning big on the film festival circuit. But we must remember that, for writers, filmmakers, talent AND investors, producing a drama screenplay involves an even bigger leap of faith, emotionally and financially, than a genre production. So what else can writers do to make their spec drama screenplays seem more appealing? For starters:

- *...Know what you're taking on.* Having a solid grasp of the writing craft is obviously a must, but, more importantly, you need to be realistic. Industry pros always stress that filmmaking is 'a marathon, not a sprint', but this only holds true if we replace human runners with SNAILS who all have arthritis (and probably dementia, too, because they periodically forget what they're doing and stand still). Apparently it took ten years for Derek Cianfrance to both write and bring us *Blue Valentine*. I don't even like to think too hard of the kinds of things going on behind the scenes there: of how many people must have chucked a spanner in the works at various times; of unexpected, random crap that happened just because it did, screwing other stuff up; or of how many times Cianfrance, his co-writers and crew thought the whole thing was more trouble than it was worth and that they should just chuck in the towel and become goat herders in the Andes, in pursuit of a more quiet life! I don't even have to know the specifics to know that's the kind of thing that happens behind EVERY produced drama.

- *...Know who you can rely on.* Dallas Buyers Club (2013) might be a multi-award-nominated and winning film now, but back in 2008 it had achieved the dubious accolade of being 'Hollywood's most stalled screenplay'. Original writer Craig Borten wrote a first draft way back in 1992, and various (great!) attachments were made throughout the rest of the nineties, all to no avail. It wasn't plain sailing, either, for *DBC*'s eventual executive producer Cassian Elwes, (who coincidentally was also co-executive producer of *Blue Valentine*). Despite having a huge list of credits to his name, Elwes revealed in his viral article, 'How I Raised the Money for *Dallas Buyers Club* in Three Days', that when he lost the investment money to make *DBC* (and not for the first time), he was officially out of options. So he sat down and figured out who really owed him... and he called in that favour. The guy who gave him the money didn't even want to do the movie! That money man believed the subject of *DBC* was 'too difficult' and there was no real market for it. But he gave Elwes the money because he owed him his own start in the business. The moral of this story? Give and you shall receive! Yes, you may not be a big shot like Elwes (yet!), but the more you give, the more likely it is that you will get the help you need – small OR big – to get your own projects off the ground, made and out there.

- *...Know that it's not all about you!* So, your great idea may indeed be fabulous (not to mention your exquisitely crafted story and characters), but you have to realise, right from the offset on a drama, that you need to 'walk the walk' as well. If you're not going to pitch and 'sell' your spec drama screenplay in the classic sense of signing on the dotted line for actual real money, you're probably going to stay with the project right from its inception through to production. This means you HAVE to be easy to work with. Remember, there are more unproduced screenplays out there than any producer or filmmaker will ever need, plus you're competing with their own ideas as well. So don't sabotage yourself by not knowing how the industry works or, worse, being a complete div. If you make someone's life difficult, s/he will walk away in a heartbeat. It really is as simple as that. So, okay, you're the writer and the idea originated with you; but it is a shared dream and thus a shared project. All films are. If you can't handle that inescapable fact, make your life, and everybody else's easier, by writing a novel instead!

With all this in mind, then, look out for what I have deemed 'selling points' at the end of each of the case studies. These are ideas for getting your own project off the ground. Whatever they suggest, they are ideas for making your spec drama screenplay happen, because the onus is on you, nobody else, to kick this off... otherwise your work is staying right where it is, on your desktop. Forever.

REASONS TO WRITE DRAMA

Make no mistake: drama has always been a hard sell. Even so, there are still reasons to consider writing one for your portfolio. Here are just some of them:

- *Challenge.* Writing a good drama screenplay is HARD. Whilst writing a genre screenplay is clearly difficult as well (hence the large number of 'misfiring' scripts in the spec pile, generally), a spec genre screenplay like horror, thriller or comedy at least has a framework of conventions to play with, not to mention a set of audience expectations to either satisfy or subvert. This might not make it 'easier', but it is at least a starting point. In comparison, a drama screenplay can be anything. Literally anything. We're talking story-wise, character-wise, or even in terms of craft elements like structure, arena, whatever! It's no wonder so many spec screenwriters' brains explode and they feel compelled to churn out stereotypical stories about clichéd characters living in sinkhole estates as standard!

- **Production.** Just like some genre screenplays, drama lends itself well to the low- and no-budget model for new filmmakers (depending what it's about, of course; it's unlikely guerrilla filmmakers will be able to stage epic battles for your war drama, though certain compromises can be made, especially if the majority of the action takes place in a siege situation, or within a trench). Also, unlike many genre screenplays that call for 'star power' (or at least recognisable faces), a spec drama screenplay makes no such demand. In fact, it's arguably BETTER if your produced drama has unknowns in it, unless you can really score with a genre star who's desperate to change his or her image; or you're lucky enough to have a big drama budget to play with that allows you to target heavyweight (read: 'award-winning') character actors.

- **Sample.** For the screenwriter yet to make his or her mark on the industry – either film or television – not to mention the established writer who perhaps has primarily worked to commission on others' ideas, the spec drama sample screenplay can offer real opportunities to shine. A genre screenplay may be excellent, but it might not suit a producer or filmmaker's particular sensibilities, leading said industry pro to question why you've sent them your blockbuster 'creature feature' or high-budget gross-out comedy when s/he specialises in stories achievable on as low a budget as possible (which, let's face it, is almost always the case in the UK!). Yet a well-written, well-conceived drama screenplay shows a scribe's ability to write believable characters and authentic scenarios, which are welcome almost everywhere. In addition, it should be noted there is a veritable dearth of good material in the spec pile in terms of realistic and emotional drama screenplays. Additionally, the majority of spec screenwriters at the moment seem to favour genre TV pilots, which seems a shame to me because feature screenplays have great currency in the industry. Many industry pros believe (rightly or wrongly) that 90+ pages is the most difficult format to tackle in terms of structure. In addition, whilst a TV producer may be just as likely to read a sample feature-length screenplay, an indie filmmaker is probably unlikely to read a sample TV pilot, which is why I always recommend features over TV pilots as samples. That said, many spec screenwriters like to flex their muscles on the structural 'strands' of returning drama – 'story of the week' versus the serial element – and if you can do this well, in an original way with characters who are not 'the usual' (i.e. 'cops 'n' docs'), your drama TV pilot is always going to stand out in the pile.

- *Catharsis.* Many writers attempt drama screenplays because they feel the story they choose will create a powerful psychological release for both them and their audience. Catharsis is definitely one of the strongest pulls of drama, but only if it is not one-sided. There must be a universal quality to one's work that the reader and viewer are able to access and relate to their own experiences. Otherwise, the writer is simply recounting their own tale of woe to a passive audience, the writing equivalent of the drunk punter going on and on at the weary bartender!

- *Prestige.* If we consider the produced content that is lauded the most in terms of awards and critics' praise, it's obvious drama is a huge winner. The more groundbreaking and 'worthy' these productions are, the better; some even achieve box-office success off the back of such acclaim. Yet making drama is still a huge risk for investors and filmmakers, especially in terms of financial return, so we must ask ourselves why they would put themselves through this. Prestige certainly plays its part: attracting awards on the film festival circuit, for example, is always a good selling point for writers and filmmakers when attempting to set up other projects. Similarly, whilst those filmmakers may have made no actual money on their drama, if you type most produced drama titles in IMDb, it soon becomes apparent that ratings are nearly always in excess of 6/10 or higher. Compare that to produced genre content, which is frequently a much patchier affair, even for Hollywood blockbusters, and which gets lower and lower for indie films, with many scoring well below 5/10, regardless of content. So it's no wonder indie filmmakers in particular are keen to chase prestige, especially via awards and festivals. One way of doing this is to build up one's reputation as a writer and/or filmmaker with short films first, leading us into our first case study.

CASE STUDY 1: THE SHORT FILM

CANCER HAIR (2014)

Writer/Director: Gail Hackston
Produced by: Isabelle Sieb, Helga Ernudottir
Budget: £15,000

Q: What's good about it?
A: Combining typical short film and drama subject matters like dating and cancer, Hackston twists audience expectations, yet still creates a story audiences can recognise and relate to. What's more, the short film brings humour as well as poignancy to a situation all of us can empathise with.

<u>MY LOGLINE:</u> A young woman, in remission from cancer and wearing a wig, attempts to go on a blind date but comes unstuck.

Writing and Selling *Cancer Hair*

Gail Hackston is a first-time writer/director. She's also a no-nonsense Scot in possession of an amiable, yet unyielding, focus. For me, she's

31

the poster girl for 'getting things done', even if that's by luck, rather than design. 'I wish I could say there was a grand plan all along, but there wasn't,' she admits.

Short filmmaking is often a 'fly by the seat of your pants' affair for filmmakers, all about grabbing opportunities and running with them, getting experience as a 'trial run' for other projects, if nothing else. But Gail's film is interesting for two reasons. *Cancer Hair* is a very ambitious and unusual project, which is arguably what makes it so compelling. 'I wanted to write something that would be relatively easy to make as my first film, was a female story and that combined shades of humour and drama,' Gail explains. 'I think so much of life is light and dark... for me, it is only when they are placed side by side that you can really see the contrast.'

Combining a date story with a cancer story may seem a strange choice to some; making it a comedy may seem practically suicidal! The cancer stories audiences most often see tend to be about the actual 'battle' with cancer, which is unsurprising. Cancer is probably the biggest adverse life event most people will undergo (especially if they die, though many cancer survivors describe cancer as 'giving more than it takes'). So depictions of cancer on screen usually focus on treatment and/or what that character must go through either to recover or to come to terms with a terminal diagnosis. Someone 'wins' and it's a triumph, or someone 'loses' and it's a tragedy. Gail's story, however, is very different: Claire is in remission, a strange time for cancer survivors that many call 'The Waiting Room', for obvious reasons, the primary fear for most being recurrence. What's more, Claire is still coming to terms with, and processing, what has happened to her, all symbolised by the loss of her hair, which is typically especially important for a woman. 'This is the "what next?"', says Gail, 'when the support systems are gone, when the person is back in "real life" and everyone is expecting them to get on with it. In Claire's case, one of those "getting on with it" things is a date.'

Dates and meetings are very commonly mined aspects of short film productions and spec screenplays. It makes the story world smaller, focusing on just two people and their reactions to each other. It's not difficult to see why it's such a popular choice for filmmakers, especially those on a low or micro-budget. 'A date has a very clear social construct that everyone indulges,' Gail says. 'You meet with someone; you have a drink or a meal; you may or may not like each other; you may or may not see each other again... I wanted my protagonist, Claire, to have one of those really godawful dates! Make her really uncomfortable, even mortify her... and watch her grow because of it.' This notion of character 'growth' is notoriously difficult to achieve in short films, especially one as short as *Cancer Hair*; just ten minutes. In short films of this length, audiences are more likely to be treated to a 'snapshot' or moment of a character's life; it's not common to see even one character undergo what I call a 'transformative arc' in the way that Claire does. Given that so many short films are autobiographical, I ask Gail whether the project has personal significance for her: are we seeing what dating was like for her, after cancer treatment? 'I have had a number of friends and family who have [had cancer],' Gail replies. 'Some have survived, some have not. Cancer is omnipresent. But it is not the black mark it once was. People survive. Some thrive. I wanted to make a hopeful film.'

So, if *Cancer Hair* is not autobiographical, I want to know how Gail came up with the idea for combining a cancer story with a date story. Gail describes two fascinating encounters that 'smashed together' in her head: 'I was having lunch with a group of people I didn't know particularly well and the woman across from me kept fidgeting with her hair,' Gail remembers. 'She was fidgeting so much that you couldn't help but look at it and see it was a wig. She was clearly upset about drawing attention to it. I felt for her and the point she was at in her life. When she went to the bathroom, some of the other women explained she was in treatment and wasn't coping well with her hair loss.' Gail goes on: 'Then, in a staff canteen, I saw another woman whose hair was growing back after chemo. No scarf, no wig, just shoulders back, shaved head and incredibly striking. She had a confidence and presence to her that just turned heads. It was amazing to watch. And massively different from the first woman.' So, as with so many stories, *Cancer Hair* for Gail started with such questions as: what causes one person to be one way and someone else another? What impact does hair loss have on a young woman? And how can she get her mojo back if she's lost it? Research is key: Gail spoke to many female cancer survivors with these questions in mind, including myself. Yet it is not a question of simply writing others' experiences, either, but combining them and creating a truthful story. Gail, who has not undergone cancer treatment or experienced the impact of hair loss impact, has achieved authenticity.

The distribution opportunities for short films have increased tenfold in the last ten years or so: there are now hundreds of film festivals and initiatives, websites and DVD compilations the low-budget drama screenplay filmmaker can take advantage of; there are even opportunities to showcase short films in pubs and at music festivals, in-between acts. Unfortunately, however, it's no more likely than it ever was for filmmakers like Gail to actually get paid for their efforts! In fact, chances are they'll be out of pocket themselves, having had to at least pay festival admin fees to be in with a chance of exhibition and/or exposure. So, with a budget of £15,000, *Cancer Hair* is an 'expensive' short film: there's a whole subgenre of micro-budget feature-length movies – especially horror and comedy – that are made for less. What's more, Gail did not access any industry help from screen agencies or similar schemes to make *Cancer Hair*. Unlike a huge proportion of guerrilla filmmakers, though, Gail did not go down the crowdfunding route. Why not? 'I hate broke filmmakers hitting up other broke filmmakers for cash,' Gail says in her usual forthright manner. 'As a marketer, I believe in creating an audience for a film first through social media, but, given the focus on cancer in the story, I had ethical reservations about asking that audience for money. So it was down to me.' So how did Gail raise the money? 'I put my hand in my own pocket,'she confesses. 'A PPI refund, some credit cards, general belt-tightening and a big push on freelance work got me there, but that route is not for the faint-hearted!' Unusually, too, Gail insisted on paying her crew and actors wherever she could, which bumped costs up even further. As Gail explains: 'For me, it was important to start as I mean to go on in the industry.'

My Take on *Cancer Hair*

As a script editor, I first came into contact with *Cancer Hair* in January 2013, when Gail Hackston, whom I'd worked with at London Screenwriters' Festival, sent me an email. She wanted me to do some notes on it, along with another screenplay, a feature-length, coming out drama spec screenplay called *The Green Door*. Gail wasn't really sure where she was with the project and had lost enthusiasm for it, she explained; she had had some confusing feedback and she wanted me to read both versions of the script that were in existence, plus the actual notes given by a short film fund. 'Oh, and by the way,' the email finished (as Gail knew I was a cancer survivor myself), 'sorry about the title!'

I don't mind admitting that, originally, I was a little peeved to receive *Cancer Hair*. After my own life-changing and traumatic experience, I found myself unusually superstitious, so getting the screenplay less than six months after finishing chemotherapy felt like some kind of bad omen. I had gone out of my way to avoid cancer stories and yet here was one, nestling in my email inbox! I almost mailed back and told Gail I couldn't read it. Luckily for Gail, however, my husband was unemployed for a short while back then, so I didn't feel able to turn down paid work... and lucky for me too, because if I had said I felt too fragile to read *Cancer Hair* I would have missed out on an extraordinary experience.

I read *The Green Door* first – and, actually, probably all of my submissions that week – before I attempted to read *Cancer Hair*. Though Gail had a downer on the project (and so did I!), I was surprised to find myself thinking that not only was it not as bad as Gail thought, but that I actively LIKED it! The two versions were quite different, especially in terms of plot beats: in one version, the protagonist's date did a runner; in the other, Claire effectively does (neither do in the finished film). Like many early drafts, the first version of the screenplay was very dialogue-led, so it felt rather theatrical; in the other draft, the arena, or 'story world', felt underserved by what was going on, especially by scene description. But neither of these were particularly problematic craft elements for a writer who is as receptive to constructive criticism as Gail. What struck me was that mysterious *je ne sais quoi*... the notion that Gail had 'got it'. The story she had chosen felt true and real to me, even though I had never been on a date when recovering from chemo. I found myself not just giving her notes, but literally telling her all my experiences: the terminal patients I had seen, cracking jokes and having a laugh, yet stopping to CONGRATULATE me on my good prognosis; how sometimes I would go out into town with my own wig on, purposefully and obviously wonky, to see if people would mention it (being British, they didn't); or how it wasn't just stares you would get, but real unbridled sympathy too. I told her about the old lady standing behind me in the post office queue who had tapped me on the shoulder and said, 'Are you okay now, dearie?' I had nodded and thanked her, and she had squeezed my arm. 'Good for you!' she said.

From there, I asked Gail how Claire felt about her future. That's what the story of *Cancer Hair* was about: it wasn't a story of recovery; it wasn't even necessarily a story about love or romance or 'starting over'. For me, it was about learning to appreciate that none of us knows how much time we have, yet still being optimistic. I believe intuition is an important part of storytelling and I trusted Gail to be able to listen to my anecdotes and experiences and 'translate' them as she saw fit on screen. This was not so she could tell MY story instead of Claire's. I think this is an element many writers mishandle when considering their own personal, lived experiences, or those of others: we must write these stories in such a way that audiences can relate to them and see themselves, relatives and/or friends reflected back at them, eliciting that all-important emotional response.

When Gail told me she was forging ahead and making *Cancer Hair* herself, I wasn't surprised. I spend a huge amount of time as a script editor counselling many of my female 'Bang2writers' to do what Gail does: make a decision and simply go for it, trusting that it will work out. This always interests me, because I don't find I have to do the same with the male Bang2writers as much... in fact, I'm often trying to hold them back! Wild horses won't keep them from making their films, whether they're ready to take the plunge or not. Yet, in comparison, women can be much more reticent about taking their filmmaking destiny into their own hands. I don't know why that is: a lack of confidence, perhaps, based on a lifetime of internalising sexist messages from society about female leadership being 'bossy' or 'bitchy'. Yet things have arguably never been better: advances in technology, plus schemes and initiatives like Bird's Eye View, Underwire and, yes, London Screenwriters' Festival, all of which nurture female talent, mean production costs are down and opportunities are increasing. What did surprise me, though, was how FAST everything was: from casting to shooting to editing to submitting for festivals, it was a matter of just a few months – but why wait around once the decision is made? As I always say on B2W, 'Want something? Go get it', and Gail certainly did that!

I was sadly unable to attend the cast and crew screening of the short up in London, so watched the finished film from the comfort of my MacBook. I'm always reticent about watching produced versions of screenplays I've consulted on and loved, because what you 'see' in your head never matches the reality, and too often this can be a disappointment. This was not the case, however, with *Cancer Hair*. Interestingly, the story kept evolving right into the edit – something unproduced spec screenwriters also constantly misjudge – and what ended up on screen is rather different from what I envisaged when it only existed on the page (and all the stronger for it). But what struck me most was Gail's flair for bright colours, aiding the optimism of the story thematically. What's more, those visuals signified how far she had come on her journey: from an underserved arena in that early draft I read, through to easily one of the most cinematic short films I'd seen in aeons. It's a massive achievement, and the reason why I'll be working with Gail Hackston on more shorts (and perhaps a feature!) in the future.

What We Can Learn from *Cancer Hair*

Write Tips:

- 'Write what you know' is very often misunderstood by spec screenwriters who believe they must write their OWN experiences only. In recent years, the phrase has been frequently disregarded by those writers who say it's invalid, citing futuristic science fiction arenas and 'larger-than-life' scenarios. In other words: you don't have to be a murderer to write great screenplays about serial killers. I prefer to take a more balanced approach and suggest writers think about 'write what you know' with reference to research. Gail has never experienced the impact of cancer and its treatment personally, yet was still able to access this world view and create an authentic depiction of Claire's journey by talking to others who HAD. However, even if Gail had undergone cancer and its successful treatment, relying on just her own experience may have meant the end result was not as successful.

- Later in this book, in the *Hours* case study, writer/director Eric Heisserer will talk about what he calls 'screenwriting mitosis': the notion of taking an idea for a story from more than one source. Gail pretty much mentions the same here, when she talks about the lady in the wig and the completely bald woman in the canteen. A key element of authentic drama, then, is taking on the experiences of many people, not just one – which makes sense, given you're trying to appeal to an audience of more than one person.

- As I frequently insist on my site and via the B2W social network, writers and filmmakers must do something different from 'the usual' in order to be in with a chance of getting noticed. Short drama screenplays about dates and cancer are ten a penny in the spec pile – but by combining the two Gail suddenly stands out. And this is the key thing to remember: standing out is not about doing something completely mad, just 'left of the middle'.

- As with many short drama screenplays (and probably just as many feature-length ones), *Cancer Hair* started off very theatrical in feel, with dialogue 'taking over'. However, having a low budget is no excuse for having a screenPLAY like this: short films deserve to be every bit as visual as their feature counterparts. Whilst drama can arguably get away with a little more dialogue than your average genre film, spec writers must remember screenwriting is still a visual medium. Often, as Gail found, it's investment in visuals via the story world that is key in bringing us the character's journey, not dialogue.

Selling Points:

- As mentioned at the beginning of this book, it's unlikely a spec screenwriter will sell even a feature-length drama screenplay the traditional way, with most projects being 'labours of love'. This is even more the case with short film. Be realistic and set yourself goals: if you have no filmmaking prowess, consider learning 'on the job' by writing and making achievable shorts first. If you really can't do that, make sure you find ways to network and make contacts with filmmakers wherever possible. Join filmmaking groups online and read filmmaking bulletins. Go to networking events and courses about filmmaking. In addition, short film is a very popular way of training media students, so contact your local college and/or university and offer your scripts. Enter competitions where the prize is to get your short film made, or find a crew for one of those 'make a short film in a weekend' challenges. In other words, leave no stone unturned!

- I'm always surprised by the number of screenwriters who insist they do not want to be directors because, as far as I'm concerned, that's the TOP way of getting noticed in indie film. Writers tend to stay away from directors, or, if they find them, screw up their chances by being too militant, especially over the problem of money (there isn't any, especially for drama). I have literally lost count of the number of times I've heard directors complain, especially about short film scripts, 'I couldn't find a decent screenplay, so in the end I just wrote it myself.' This is crazy and suggests the following: i) writers need to find some directors, pronto, in the ways I described in the previous section, or ii) there need to be more writer-directors, whose actual PURPOSE is directing AND writing, rather than just writing out of necessity. Pick one of these and DO IT... it is seriously your way in. Stop looking a gift horse in the mouth!

- As a writer and director, Gail thought long and hard about her goals and how to get there. As she wants to build a career (rather than just make a one-off film), it was important to her to pay those involved in helping her. That's not to say that collaborations are wrong: many people work for free in the industry, for different reasons and with different objectives (some of them good and some of them bad). Certainly, had Gail asked for people to do this gratis, she would not have been short of offers. On the same basis, when thinking about raising the money for *Cancer Hair*, she gave a lot of consideration to what she considered 'ethical', especially given the subject matter. With all this in mind, Gail decided to self-fund, rather than pursue avenues like crowdfunding. That path isn't possible for everyone, of course – especially not to the tune of £15,000! – but perhaps there is an argument to be made for filmmakers NOT automatically using crowdfunding when there are so many projects competing for attention; or at least for them to use it in a more informed way.

- Whilst it's true that there are many distribution opportunities for short films in terms of film festivals, there's a whole other industry dedicated to getting your film into the most prestigious ones. What's more, it's not always clear why your film has been rejected, even if you've paid your money to an advisor to help you. In short: there are acres of GREAT shorts that have never seen the light of day at a film festival, and this is certainly not because their makers haven't tried, often parting with their hard-earned cash.

So don't pin all your hopes on film festivals; think beyond them from the outset. What other opportunities are out there for your short drama? Identify your own: if your short drama story features a female protagonist or people of colour, why not target filmmakers accordingly? Then you can pinpoint funding opportunities, festivals and similar schemes on that basis. Scour the trades and keep a close eye out online for appeals for submissions to short film nights at café bars, pubs and universities or other venues. Why not stage your own short film night, using it as a further opportunity to network? If you have website building skills, why not create a whole site for your drama screenplay or produced film, creating pages dedicated to 'behind the scenes', including a PDF of the screenplay, and send the link to friends who are teachers and lecturers in creative writing or English? Why not visit schools and youth groups and show the short film, followed by a Q&A session?

- Later in the book, *Dear Frankie*'s screenwriter Andrea Gibb will posit the notion that she has seen NO difference between the ability of female directors and their male counterparts to do their jobs. I totally agree: gender is no barrier whatsoever to talent as far as I'm concerned. Yet go-getting types like Gail Hackston, who make their own opportunities and run with them, are still relatively rare in my experience. And whilst it's certainly true that the industry can be sexist (especially at the 'higher' levels, i.e. awards and certain funding and distribution opportunities), there is absolutely nothing to physically stop more women from doing what Gail has done – a self-funded short film. Obviously not everyone has £15,000 to spare, especially women who are mothers and not working, or are raising children on their own. Yet there are still FREE opportunities to network and create with other people on micro or no budgets that women just aren't always taking advantage of. We have to ask ourselves why this is in an attempt to address it wherever we can – and by 'we', I mean men too. All of us need to be the allies of women in film so that we can break this cycle, once and for all.

TRUTH AND DARE

DRAMA AND TRUTH

In recent years, 'drama' has become a bit of a dirty word, especially for distributors, but, as we know, it's still very much part of the industry and most likely always will be. Read the trades and you'll see oodles of drama features being made, with many winning big at film festivals and/or high-profile awards ceremonies. Often the most beloved and enduring movies will be dramas, with true stories scoring especially high, as seen in the IMDb list in the previous section. So, low-budget drama offers new and/or penniless spec screenwriters a significant 'foot in the door' by way of short film and transmedia strategies, especially web series, which can also win awards as well as recognition. But first we need to define what drama 'really' is, if we are to write our own spec drama screenplays.

DRAMA, A DEFINITION

We all have our own ideas on what makes 'good' drama. In attempting to create it, we will package any number of storytelling devices and elements to induce a response in our desired target audience. For the purposes of this book, however, it would be advantageous in the first instance to pin down exactly what I mean by 'drama screenplays' so we can all begin on the same page, quite literally. So, to me, drama screenplays are:

- **Low-budget.** Budgets, especially in the UK, have got lower and lower in this age of austerity. It is not uncommon to make genre films like comedies and horrors for between £100,000 and £300,000 all in, for example. In contrast, some of the produced drama case studies in this book may seem high-budget, the two highest being *Dear Frankie*, weighing in at approximately £2 million, and *Saving Mr Banks*, coming in at a whopping £35 million. What's important to remember here is context: *Dear Frankie* was made with screen agency support, at a time when budgets and film funding had not been cut as severely as they have now; and, in the case of the latter, £35 million isn't a lot of money (really!) to Hollywood. As a first-time writer or filmmaker, your chances of raising in excess of £200,000 for your drama screenplay are extremely small, so knowing what is possible for that kind of money is absolutely essential.

- **'Small' stories.** Drama screenplays are usually deeply personal stories about a single issue that nevertheless have a universal quality, meaning something to their target audience and, in some cases, beyond. Drama stories carry something 'recognisable' about them, so audiences can see reflections of their own lived experiences within the story, meaning dramas about growing up, cancer, abuse, addiction, love, relationship breakdowns and parenting are extremely popular. However, even in the case of 'big' subject matter like war, the viewpoint in a produced drama is usually personal too and does not take in the conflict as a whole.

- **Emotional.** Drama movies, whether feature-length or short, are designed to provoke an emotional response in the audience, the most common being pathos. However, the best drama stories are not one-note. They include a range of emotions, so there are moments of light as well as shade.

- **Authentic.** Authenticity is crucial in all storytelling, but in comparison to genre film, in which characters must be seen to DO authentic actions, drama characters must be authentic in terms of their emotional responses. Writers are essentially rendering their characters' psychology, as well as their actions, in drama, which is why writing a drama screenplay is so difficult. I will return to this notion in the section entitled 'What is Emotional Truth?'

- *Realistic.* Dramas are typically set in the 'real world', even when they employ obvious artifice like period drama *12 Years a Slave* (2013), or an 'unreal-real world' like the film set on the moon in *The Truman Show* (1998). Dramas usually do not make use of highly stylised filmmaking technique or tone, adopting as close to a 'real-life feel' as possible, though there are obvious exceptions: mockumentary, as in *It's All Gone Pete Tong* (2004); non-linearity, as in *(500) Days of Summer* (2009); or cinéma-vérité, such as *End of Watch* (2012).

- *About 'struggle'.* The word most often associated with 'drama' is 'depressing', but I believe great drama stories are not depressing (and will go into more detail as to why in this book). Also, where does optimistic fare like *Juno* (2007) or *Little Miss Sunshine* (2006) fit in? Even stories with devastating resolutions like *Brokeback Mountain* may still include hope for the future. On this basis, I posit the notion that 'real' drama (as opposed to 'genre') is about STRUGGLE, not necessarily pathos.

My definition of drama, then, is this:

> *A personal, realistic and authentic story about the internal conflict and struggles of a character, so that we might appreciate their world view, specifically their psyche.*

The main idea of drama is that the audience can relate their own experiences to those of the character, which in turn elicits an emotional response. Or, to put it bluntly: good dramas are about THOUGHTS and FEELINGS – the characters' AND the audience's!

WHAT IS 'EMOTIONAL TRUTH'?

We can hopefully all name the main emotions, but 'What is truth?' is a philosophical question argued over for centuries and never yet answered to all of humanity's satisfaction (and nor could it be). When thinking about audience response to produced drama content and a filmmaker's desire to create that response in the first place, though, I'd venture 'emotional truth' is primarily about placing honesty and integrity of emotion at the heart of the story, via the following:

• *Authenticity.* Though it will, of course, depend on the story being told, certain elements of ALL stories must create opportunities for the audience to imagine themselves in the characters' places and/or relate the characters' actions to their own lived experiences and/or knowledge. Though it is neither possible nor desirable for a screenplay of any kind to recreate a character's journey or actions EXACTLY as they would be in 'real life', audiences still have to be able to suspend their disbelief; the events and actions of the characters have to feel 'right', never deviating from authenticity. This doesn't mean drama screenplays can't sacrifice facts for the sake of drama, and it's certainly true that most dramas will not please everyone. Arguably, then, the notion of authenticity and emotional truth comes down to writer and filmmaker intention: we are, to quote producer of *Rob Roy* (1995) and *The Flying Scotsman* (2006), Peter Broughan, 'telling lies to tell the truth'.

• *Passion.* Ever been told your story is derivative? I think everyone has at least once – or will be at some point – and scribes often get insulted, believing they are being accused of 'ripping off' stories already in existence. Whilst this may be true as well, I've found that, when it comes to drama screenplays, the problem is generally to do with a lack of emotion or 'passion' in the piece, usually because the writer has concentrated more on the craft elements of the script than the story and characters at its heart. It's possible even for complete messes of screenplays to be full of passion and emotional truth; more than once I've ended up working with a writer who is largely inexperienced but has poured his/her heart and soul into a piece so on the button that the producer in question has asked them through the door regardless! The key here is ensuring that you master the screenwriting craft, whilst maintaining the passion or fire the story lit under you and which made you want to tell it in the first place. If you let that spark go out, in the course of multiple redrafts and countless rejections, your drama screenplay is sunk.

- *Pain.* Pain is one of the driving forces of human endeavour: avoiding pain; confronting pain; dealing with pain. So it makes sense that great drama often comes from a place of pain, both for the writers and the characters within those stories. Recognition of shared pain brings people together and helps them heal, which is a massive motivator for filmmaking teams to want to make certain drama screenplays... and for audiences to want to see them. In contrast, the pain of marginalised sections of society can educate the majority, making them think, perhaps for the first time, about those people's lives and difficulties that most have disregarded up until now.

But, again, 'real' drama isn't just about pain or one long misery fest; there should be light as well as shade, humour as well as tears... but this is what a very large number of writers forget, unfortunately. As already outlined, I believe drama is 'a personal, realistic and authentic story about the internal conflict and struggles of a character, so that we might appreciate their world view, specifically their psyche', and one recent movie that did this especially well in my view is the one I've chosen as the second case study of this book.

CASE STUDY 2: THE TRUE STORY

SAVING MR BANKS (2013)

Written by: Kelly Marcel, Sue Smith
Directed by: John Lee Hancock
Produced by: Alison Owen
Budget: $35 million

Q: What's good about it?

A: It features a female anti-heroine with her own rigid world view AND agenda, yet still manages to make us not only understand her reasons, but empathise with her too.

MY LOGLINE: The story behind the battle of wills between Walt Disney and author PL Travers over the rights to and adaptation of her classic novel, *Mary Poppins*.

Writing and Selling *Saving Mr Banks*

Saving Mr Banks is one of those rare beasts: a British, female-led, female-centric true story (that's also non-linear!), involving copyrighted material, by one of the biggest studios in Hollywood. There must have been many in the movie's journey who declared *Saving Mr Banks* to be an 'impossible task', yet here it is and it's not difficult to see why. PL Travers was both a talented and fascinating woman, seemingly years ahead of her time: deeply spiritual, she studied Buddhism, was an actress and even had affairs with women. Yet, as is so often the case with true stories about real people, choices had to be made regarding what to include in the story. 'So much of her life was colourful and challenging and fascinating, but we chose simply to tell the story of two weeks she spent in Los Angeles in 1961,' says co-writer Kelly Marcel. In the spec pile, dramas that are true stories often falter: they simply include far too much, muddying the story, message or theme and the characters' motivations. So whilst some viewers of *Saving Mr Banks* may have felt frustration at the depiction of PL Travers, it's important to note we can see only a 'snapshot' of her and her experiences of those two weeks spent with Disney himself. 'Movies are windows into a special experience that one person had – an experience that holds universal relevance for us all,' Kelly says. This notion of 'universal relevance' is what many spec drama screenplays get horrendously wrong, especially when the scribe in question is writing an autobiographical screenplay, or s/he hangs on to the notion that, because certain events 'really happened', they should be included. But this is not possible when creating what is, in essence, fiction. 'When you write the story of someone's life, you're not actually writing the story of their life,' explains Kelly. 'It's not possible or desirable.' This does not mean that spec drama screenplay writers can do what they like with a true story, though: 'There is no carte blanche to be taken because there are people, relatives of Pamela and Disney, still living and to whom we owe integrity,' Kelly asserts, quite rightly.

Now one of Hollywood's hottest screenwriters (after a decade's worth of 'overnight success'!), Marcel is the daughter of cult writer/ director Terry Marcel, becoming an actress at the age of three, when she was eaten by an alien in one of her father's films. Many bit parts followed, though she never enjoyed acting and 'retired' in her mid twenties, deciding to become a screenwriter instead. Though she did do an uncredited rewrite on prison biopic *Bronson* (2008), *Saving Mr Banks* is, officially, Marcel's first film. Kelly met with Alison Owen from Ruby Films about the project in 2010; there was a previous script by Sue Smith about PL Travers' relationship with her adopted son (who, interestingly, later became an alcoholic like Travers' own father). However, Alison felt she wanted to tell a different story and was, Kelly tells me, immediately hooked, recounting how *Mary Poppins* (1964) had been a Christmas tradition in her house growing up, going on to say: 'It fascinated me that [Mary Poppins], with talking umbrella and daisy-decorated hat, was born from so much pain.'

It's perhaps this notion of personal pain that drives *Saving Mr Banks*: PL Travers is a tortured individual, desperate to hang on to her beloved Mary for personal reasons. She is also the character the audience perhaps knows least about. Her story is not what we expect, and we are party to the machinations of her psyche in a way the other characters in the movie are not. This is why PL Travers is the protagonist of the film, rather than the antagonist – a version which would have cast Disney as the hero instead, clawing the *Mary Poppins* rights from a troublesome and hysterical artiste. 'I didn't think Walt's version was that interesting. He wanted something, someone was being difficult about him getting it, the end,' Kelly declares. 'I preferred the idea that the audience knew something he didn't.'

Moving on from the true nature of the story, then, we must consider its non-linearity. How difficult was it to structure? 'Non-linear storytelling is a bugger,' Kelly says frankly. 'It's really hard to find a rhythm and a feel for where the transitions should be when you're dealing with two timelines.' *Saving Mr Banks* contrasts PL Travers' 'present' with flashbacks of her difficult childhood that act as an elucidation of the various choices our author makes in her battle of wills with Walt Disney. A key element of the present-day thread's journey, however, is Ralph, PL Travers' driver, an entirely fictional creation of Marcel's who plays a vital role in the story, helping the audience understand PL Travers. 'I don't know where Ralph came from. He just popped into my head one day. Sometimes you just pull the right balloon down from the ceiling,' Kelly smiles.

Now consider the most troublesome element of *Saving Mr Banks* – the fact that it takes in copyrighted material, the actual adapted movie of *Mary Poppins*. Permissions for things like songs and movies can run into hundreds of thousands of pounds, yet Disney as a corporation is also known to be fiercely protective of its beloved founder. Could a 'bunch of women from London' really create a story involving Walt himself? The answer to that is, of course, evident, because not only did Marcel, Smith and Owen satisfy Disney, the studio actually came on board in making the picture. Remembering that initial meeting with Alison Owen, it would seem Kelly's gut instinct about the project was right: 'It was one of those meetings that you very rarely have, where you just "know" you absolutely have to do a project. Money or no money,' she says. Sometimes, belief in a story's potency and its ability to 'speak' to an audience is all you need.

My Take on *Saving Mr Banks*

PL Travers behaves in a frequently ghastly way throughout the 'present-day' thread of *Saving Mr Banks*. We might have expected our author to be the antagonist instead, getting lambasted by this storyline (or at least the characters around her) for her behaviour, especially given the overt sexism of the period it is set in, not to mention the latent misogyny of the film industry in general. Instead, both brittle and sharp, Travers for me brings to mind Melvin Udall in *As Good As It Gets* (1997). There is the same kind of incredulous disbelief reserved for her most brazen moments, and even a bizarre sympathy for her unreasonable disgust at discovering a giant Mickey Mouse toy on her bed in her hotel room, a gift from Disney himself! Later in the film, we again find ourselves feeling sorry for her as, feeling lonely, she takes the toy into bed with her for a cuddle. This is especially refreshing for a female protagonist, as these are frequently cast against troublesome men, in both the spec pile and produced content, as if women are all automatically 'nice' (!) or, conversely, two-dimensional 'bitches'.

As anyone who has read the original book or seen the movie realises, Mary Poppins as a character feels quintessentially 'English', so it is perhaps surprising that *Saving Mr Banks* begins not in the UK (or even the US), but Australia. It's here that PL Travers – or 'Ginty' – grew up. The family's real surname was Goff, with Ginty the eldest of three children. All of them were ruled over by the whimsical, yet tortured, alcoholic father figure, Travers Goff, whose Christian name our author will take as her pseudonym in later years. Ginty's mother, Margaret, was young and put-upon, hoping for the best but too often getting the worst of her husband's excesses; her life the epitome of the triumph of hope over bitter experience. Despite this, Ginty appears to see her mother as a killjoy and possibly even a usurper, getting between her and her father, whom she adores. Ginty's close relationship with her father is painted in glorious Technicolor from the outset, but it is important to note it is not a relationship built on emotional or sexual abuse. Instead, Ginty is Travers' favourite child and her father is quite literally our author's world. It is Travers who captures and inspires Ginty's imagination, but more than that, in those moments he is the father ANY child would wish for. Travers is heavily idealised, with eyes only for Ginty, the other two children (or, indeed, Margaret) barely getting a look in.

However, as the flashbacks become ever more tragic, PL Travers' steadfast resolve in the present thread begins to unravel. We see chinks in her armour and begin to understand not only why she acts the way she does, but how she might have turned out had her father not died... or, rather, had she been able to 'save' him, like she can the fictional Mr Banks (who appears in both *Mary Poppins* the novel and its subsequent screen adaptation). In the past-tense thread, it becomes apparent Travers is set on self-destruction as his alcoholism becomes more and more out of control. It is his death that creates a void in our author she is never truly able to fill, especially as she blames herself for his loss. Believing her mother to be withholding alcohol from Travers out of spite, Ginty brings him a bottle, thus sealing his fate. Soon after, there is an impressive moment when Margaret appears at Ginty's bedroom door in only her nightdress, her face full of incredulous disbelief and horror at her eldest child's betrayal. But she says none of this, instead telling Ginty to look after her sisters (suggesting Ginty should take Margaret's place as the matriarch; she has been the 'other woman' in Margaret and Travers' marriage, essentially). Margaret then walks out of the family homestead into the darkness, barefoot, forcing Ginty to follow on horseback, calling for her mother to return. Heartbroken, Margaret appears unable to hear her daughter, wading into the creek as if to drown herself. Ginty plunges in after her, grabbing her mother; Margaret finally comes to her senses and the two of them are reconciled, hugging, still in the water. Margaret realises she must take her family back; Travers is dying and she will be the only parent. She cannot leave this to Ginty.

After this turning point, Margaret calls her sister, the children's Aunt Ellie, to help. Immediately the parallels between Aunt Ellie and Mary Poppins are obvious: like the fictional character, Aunt Ellie appears dressed in black, wearing a large brimmed hat and sporting a carpet bag. She is efficient and organised, ensuring the children realise their own places in helping their mother. During her stay, Travers inevitably dies and Margaret wishes to shield Ginty from this, but it is Ellie who insists the child must see the body. Ginty views her dead father, appreciating for the first time the gravity of her actions in giving him that final bottle of alcohol, but we get the impression our author will spend a lifetime processing this, which relates brilliantly to the struggle PL Travers finds herself in with Disney via the 'present' thread.

Being a true story, one of the biggest threats to the audience's suspension of disbelief is the fact we all KNOW Travers must have signed the agreement, because *Mary Poppins* is an adapted movie we have all at least heard about (being one of the most famous in the Disney canons). This means the stakes in the present-day thread are called into question from the offset, which is why the addition of the past thread is so necessary. What's more, as PL Travers is – at least on the surface – so disagreeable a character, the audience wants an insight into why she's the way she is, especially given there are moments in the present-day thread where her motives seem at odds with her resulting or previous behaviour. This is illustrated best when examining her relationship with Ralph (played to perfection by a scene-stealing Paul Giamatti), the driver she is assigned by Disney when she travels over to the US. Ralph, a fictional creation by writer Kelly Marcel, provides the audience with the tools to see past PL Travers' brittle, and even sometimes nasty, exterior. Ralph is a simple man, yet makes keen observations with a childlike logic that is strangely compelling. Ralph is the catalyst for two crucial moments in which Travers is forced to question her cynicism, not only about Disney, but about her fellow man in general: first, when he joins her, without a second's thought, digging in the ground outside the studio; and, second, when he meets his hero, Walt Disney, for this enables our author to see Disney through Ralph's eyes and appreciate, finally, the joy Disney is able to bring his audiences, even if she does not care for Disney's films herself. This leads later to her giving Ralph a signed book for his disabled daughter, Jane, telling him that just because Jane has problems does not mean she cannot achieve. Here, PL Travers is, in essence, returning the favour for the insights Ralph himself has given her during her stay in America.

Female characters are too often 'likeable' characters in produced content, yet PL Travers proves that a complicated, irascible and ultimately disagreeable character can not only work (regardless of gender), but that we can still relate to her. *Saving Mr Banks* took on a gargantuan task, both in attempting to bring such a character to the big screen in the first place, and in the story itself. As Kelly Marcel freely admits, there was only one studio that could have produced the movie: Disney itself! Had Disney not wanted to get involved, the whole project would have been dead in the water. But the team at Ruby Films did not let this sabotage their aspirations. They pushed ahead and were rewarded handsomely for it, which is as it should be, for the movie will undoubtedly become a classic, just like its predecessor *Mary Poppins*.

What We Can Learn from *Saving Mr Banks*

Write Tips:

- Pain may be the factor by which an audience comes to understand a character, as we do with PL Travers; but, crucially, we are not reminded of this every second of the movie. PL Travers is brusque, infuriating, even funny at times; she does not sit by a window weeping copiously about the tragic loss of her father when she was a child. Instead, this is hinted at by cleverly constructed motifs, such as the pears, which remind her of her father's death.

- Remember that the characterisation of female protagonists is often underplayed in both spec and produced content. An unusual and seemingly paradoxical character like PL Travers may gain your drama screenplay attention in the marketplace BUT only if you balance her rare qualities against those we can readily recognise.

- Non-linear movies must 'restructure their structure' so the narrative thread(s) dealing with past events support the story being told in the present; flashbacks and their like mustn't simply fill in gaps, or be disjointed for the sake of it.

- Why not try writing TWO outlines and/or scene breakdowns: one dealing with the present, the other the past? THEN weave them together to make up the whole.

- Assess whether your drama screenplay really needs to be non-linear: what does the addition of non-linearity bring? It cannot be just style over substance.

- Remember that being faithful to the story and characters does not necessarily mean you have to recreate every single event, person or thing exactly as it happened. Whilst you 'owe' something to the person (or their loved ones) whose life you are rendering as image, faithfulness is more about emotional truth.

Selling Points:

- One of the biggest challenges of writing and selling true stories as drama screenplays is that audiences potentially already know the outcome of the situation we are writing about: so instead think, 'How can I bring new insights to that true story?' In the case of *Saving Mr Banks*, the audience would probably expect it to be Disney's story, but instead the focus is on why PL Travers behaved the way she did, with an insight into the tragic loss of her father and why *Mary Poppins* means so much to her.

- Costing approximately £35 million, *Saving Mr Banks* has the highest budget of all the produced dramas in this book. Watching the movie, it's not difficult to see why. Adding to the bill are a large cast, including child actors and animals; period costumes and locations in three different countries; crowd scenes; and singing and dancing. But it's important to note that £35 million is NOT that great an amount to a studio like Disney, who funded *Bridge to Terabithia* (2007) for a similar amount, albeit with no real stars. On this basis, if you think your drama screenplay could appeal to a studio or network (like Film 4), by all means go for it – but you will need a really compelling story to get a meeting, never mind a read request. But, hey, anything is possible, as Ruby Films showed here!

- Generally speaking, including copyrighted material in your screenplay – movies, books, songs, imagery, and so on – adds thousands (sometimes hundreds of thousands) to the budget and should be avoided. However, there are always special cases: *Saving Mr Banks* arguably could not have been told to its fullest potential without including material from *Mary Poppins*. So if you feel you have to include copyrighted material in your spec drama screenplay, make sure there is a valid STORY reason for it.

- Sometimes a story will just 'speak' to you and you will find yourself unable to stop thinking about it. So be brave like Kelly Marcel, Sue Smith and Ruby Films. They let nothing – not even copyrighted material! – get in the way of their vision... and their steadfast resolve and belief in the project brought Disney itself on board.

THE PSYCHE AND CONFLICT

EMOTIONAL RESPONSE

If 'eliciting an emotional response' is the 'point' of drama, it could be argued the point of ALL stories is to do this, genre OR drama! Horrors are designed to horrify us; thrillers to thrill; comedies to make us laugh. Even a martial arts movie with a paper-thin plot and characters to match is designed to excite us, at the very least. So it's important to note that it's not so much the *type* of emotion inspired by a drama as the way it is brought forth. Whilst genre pieces may ask us to imagine ourselves in characters' places, dramas invite us to see into the character's psyche and world view, and why that is causing conflict in their lives for some reason. Whilst spec screenwriters are often comfortable with the notion of conflict being driven by a character with some sort of goal (usually because s/he 'wants or needs something'), what they don't always appreciate is that a drama character's goal, need or want is frequently 'internal', whereas a genre character's is 'external.' But how do they differ?

INTERNAL VERSUS EXTERNAL CONFLICT

When it comes to characterisation in ANY screenplay, it's certainly true that, in most stories, it's desirable to have a character who wants something and/or has a specific need or goal, leading to their being pitted against certain obstacles in their struggle to achieve it (including, but not limited to, an antagonist character). This causes many writers to question the notion of 'character-led drama'. What does it mean? Perhaps the most straightforward way of figuring out the differences between drama and genre films is by thinking not of their stories as a whole, but of the conflict that underpins them. Is it internal or external – does it come from within your characters, or from an outside situation? The difference is as follows:

- **Internal conflict.** Many writers believe drama to be a genre in its own right, especially as the word 'genre' essentially means 'category', as defined by the dictionary. Regardless of what writers feel, however, the key here is not so much what the word literally means, as how the actual industry sees it. As I've already described, drama films are often realistic, personal stories that place emotion and authenticity at their hearts; this means protagonists are frequently the ones driving the action, which comes from within them. This is what is meant by a story being 'character-led'.

- **External conflict.** In direct contrast, then, genre films are more frequently event-driven, pulling their protagonists into situations in which they are FORCED to react for some reason. In addition, the stakes are often literal in genre film, most commonly life-or-death, especially in the cases of horror and thriller. But even when risk of actual death is not present (such as in comedy), there will be some 'outside' element like a deadline, meaning there is a specific risk of loss to the characters, such as losing their home, job, spouse or face (as in humiliation) – sometimes all of these. In addition, genre films will utilise specific conventions to confirm AND break with audience expectation, which may relate to specific characters and storytelling techniques. For example, in creature thriller *Pitch Black* (2000) we are asked to invest in the journey of Fry, so may reasonably assume she will survive to the end as the so-called 'final girl'. When she does not, we are shocked.

With the above in mind, then, the industry sees genre film at grass-roots level as something that is high-concept – or, rather, event-driven – with high (often literal) stakes, which utilises stylised storytelling that's highly commercial for a mass audience. In contrast, the industry sees drama film as everything that is NOT that (yet which may include life-or-death stakes too). Remember, drama is typically about the minutiae of life and will probably include events and situations everyone in the audience will have direct or indirect experience of, such as relationships, illness, or family problems. This means a drama story and its characters need to be truthful, so audiences can relate to them. Yet still many spec screenwriters struggle with making their spec drama screenplays authentic and relevant, probably because the notion of 'drama concept' is notoriously slippery to pin down, especially when it comes to theme.

WHAT IS THEME?

If 'high-concept' means a story that is event-driven with literal stakes, writers could be forgiven for believing the opposite would be so-called 'low-concept'! Instead, however, it is more advantageous to think of it as the aforementioned 'character-led drama'. Most commonly, a character looks inside him or herself and must change his/her life in some way, for a particular reason (which may include literal life-or-death stakes, or may be metaphorical instead; sometimes it is both). The dictionary calls 'theme' a 'unifying or dominant idea, motif' and produced dramas are often overtly concerned with a message (moral or otherwise), whereas this should arguably be secondary in genre film (or needn't play a part at all). Genre film may utilise very obvious and/or generic themes, such as 'good versus evil' or 'survival of the fittest', calling into play various wide elements the audience may interpret based on their own world view. Again in contrast, many produced dramas may attempt to communicate more overtly and specifically with their target audiences, so they may be cautionary tales, or challenging or inspirational stories, and/or they may be groundbreaking, usually by being the first project to represent or combine certain story elements, especially with regard to social issues or subjects, or characters from marginalised groups not usually seen in mainstream cinema.

COMMON THEMES IN PRODUCED DRAMA

This is by no means an exhaustive list and there will be many produced dramas that exist simultaneously on several platforms, especially thematically. However, breaking down produced dramas, I was rather surprised to discover that, despite there being a wide selection of stories in terms of execution, all the ones I could think of fitted into four broad categories in terms of theme:

- *Morality.* The 'right thing' is something mined by many stories regardless of whether they are drama or genre, though dramas will frequently utilise literary techniques like allegory, allusion and dramatic irony to make their points. Though *District 9* (2009) was presented primarily as a science fiction thriller, it could be argued this allegory for apartheid was in fact more of a drama as its horrified protagonist Wikus van de Merwe finds himself 'in league with the beasts' and thus forced to understand them, further underlining the moral message that 'xenophobia is wrong'. *Quiz Show* (1994), the story of the fraud scandal that rocked the popular 1950s TV show *Twenty One*, used allusions to Shakespeare amongst others via its dialogue to bolster its message that 'cheating is wrong' (by contrast, it should be noted 'homage' is usually a visual choice of the director and/or cinematographer's, rather than the screenwriter's). Finally, dramatic irony may be employed in certain produced dramas to give the target audience a sense of doom and/or the 'inevitable', especially a character being (usually) his own worst enemy, i.e. 'had the character not done X, Y would not have subsequently happened'. We can see this most obviously in *Harsh Times* (2005): had Jim never rejected his pregnant girlfriend or smoked the marijuana in the set-up, his death may have been preventable in the resolution, the message being irresponsibility should not (and will not) be rewarded in life.

- *Truth.* The pursuit of truth 'no matter what' is the focal point of many produced dramas. However, in comparison with thrillers that may place a conspiracy or problem at the heart of the story for a protagonist to figure out, a produced drama often takes in other elements such as 'identity' or 'redemption' to do this. In 'identity' stories, characters may investigate themselves to discover the 'truth' of who they are and what they need, as in coming of age and/or coming out stories such as *My Own Private Idaho* (1991) or *What's Eating Gilbert Grape* (1993). In 'redemption' stories, characters with dark pasts may find something that delivers them to something better, probably exemplified best by the (non-horror or fantasy) work of Stephen King and subsequent movie adaptations like *The Shawshank Redemption* (1994).

- *Responsibility.* Being responsible for another human being weighs heavy, so it's no accident parenthood features strongly in this type of produced drama, as does sibling rivalry: a movie like *You Can Count on Me* (2000) personifies both these elements. However, other different kinds of responsibility stories may appear, such as a lawyer or investigator's desire to get justice and/or answers for a violated client, as in *The Accused* (1988), *A Time To Kill*, (1996) or *The General's Daughter* (1999). Alternatively, that investigator may be keen for a defendant to admit responsibility in an ambiguous case in which it is not immediately apparent exactly who (or indeed what) is at fault, as in *The Life of David Gale* (2003) or *The Exorcism of Emily Rose* (2005).

- *Enlightenment.* It is common for characters in produced dramas to have realisations and thus transform their outlook on a particular issue; sometimes their entire world view is altered by the experiences they undergo in the story. Frequently a character with an incredible talent will be the focus of a drama featuring enlightenment, such as the eponymous janitor of *Good Will Hunting* (1997), who is a mathematical genius. Also a pathological liar and unable to relate to authority, Will goes into therapy to avoid jail time, though all his psychologists sack him until he meets with Sean. The two men bond over their shared past experiences – both have survived child abuse – with the older man finally enabling Will to accept the abuse was not his fault. Jobs feature heavily in this type of drama, particularly with characters going into war zones and other cultures, either as soldiers or civilians. In *Hotel Rwanda* (2004), when war breaks out between the Hutu and Tutsi tribes, a Hutu hotelier initially cares only for the safety of his family and the maintaining of his business. As the narrative continues, however, inspired by his own marriage to a Tutsi, he attempts to save as many of his countrymen as he can from genocide, regardless of their tribe. Another example is *The Last King of Scotland* (2006), where fictional Scottish doctor Nicholas Garrigan relates how he became (the real) Ugandan dictator Idi Amin's personal physician. Garrigan is fascinated by the colourful Amin but is forced to see the negative impact he has on his country.

As 'enlightenment' is arguably one of the most common themes in produced drama content, I thought I would use it for our third case study, albeit an example much smaller and closer to home: *Dear Frankie*.

CASE STUDY 3: THE ENLIGHTENMENT STORY

DEAR FRANKIE (2004)

Written by: Andrea Gibb
Directed by: Shona Auerbach
Produced by: Gillian Berrie
Budget: £2.3 million

Q: What's good about it?

A: Placing a 'silent' character at the heart of the story, this movie makes impressive (and justified) use of voiceover, exploring how children are perhaps not as in need of protection from reality as their parents might think.

MY LOGLINE: A single mother writes letters to her son, pretending they are from his dad, who she says is away at sea. When 'his' ship docks in their town, however, she is forced to hire a stranger to play the role of Frankie's father.

Writing and Selling *Dear Frankie*

Dear Frankie started off life not as a feature, but as a 13-minute/page short film that was shortlisted for the Tartan Shorts scheme with Scottish Screen. Though it was commended, it didn't get made. 'So I just kind of forgot about it and did other things,' says the film's writer, Andrea Gibb. Then, out of nowhere, she received an email from a producer, asking Andrea if she had anything suitable for a new director, Shona Auerbach, who was 'up and coming'. And not only that – the prodco actually had money! 'It wasn't that long ago, but it was a different age back then,' Andrea says wistfully. Andrea is right: as with *Beautiful Thing* in 1996, it's unlikely a spec drama screenplay – or indeed ANY spec screenplay – would have a budget as high as *Dear Frankie*'s nowadays. Happily, however, the development process for *Dear Frankie* is typical, even if, these days, scribes (and producers!) are more likely to have to fund their passion projects themselves. Andrea collaborated with the producers to develop *Dear Frankie* from 13 to 90 minutes. 'The short film was set in the sixties,' Andrea explains. 'I grew up around that time, plus I wanted to exclude modern technology, such as email.' This changed in development, however. Nevertheless, though *Dear Frankie* is set 'today', it has a timeless quality; its set dressing, the costumes, the way it's shot, the colours used all mean it can be interpreted as being set in the past as well. 'It has this lovely kind of fable aspect,' Andrea says.

It was during the development process that Andrea won a script reading, with actors, at the Edinburgh Film Festival. 'I can recommend all writers do a script reading,' Andrea says. 'There's no quicker or more effective way of finding out what's working and what's not.' An actress once herself, Andrea understands the ability of her colleagues to breathe life into characters, not just on set, but long before that: 'I like to write for particular actors, it helps me,' says Andrea. 'Of course, it doesn't always turn out that way and whoever I cast in my head is not always who ends up on screen. But visualising a real person can, I think, give your mind access to extra details.' So did any of the people she cast in her mind's eye end up in *Dear Frankie*? 'No,' Andrea laughs, 'but Shona's casting was empathetic to the story. Gerard (Butler) was just brilliant as The Stranger, so restrained. Emily Mortimer was incredible; her discipline and intelligence were just so good. And the boy! His eyes... they instinctively understood what we were trying to do. All the actors brought something extra, something more than I hoped for.'

Frankie's deafness is such an integral part of the story in the feature, so I was surprised when Andrea explained Frankie was not deaf in the original short film script. 'I needed a reason for him living inside his head,' Andrea says, 'otherwise, why wouldn't he and his mother speak?' This element of the screenplay sounds as if it was one of those light-bulb moments, where everyone in the development process asked themselves incredulously, 'Why didn't we think of this before??' (I've found this myself as a script editor: that the best ideas often reveal themselves in this manner.) But it wasn't just a question of simply 'making' Frankie deaf. Realism was important to everyone on *Dear Frankie* and Andrea did copious amounts of research and workshops with the deaf community in Glasgow. Shona Auerbach even had a signer on set for the shoot.

What's very striking about *Dear Frankie* is not only how 'woman-centric' the story is as a tale of motherhood (rather than the more neutral notion of 'parenthood'), but how many women were involved in the actual production, too. 'Women have been very significant to my career,' Andrea acknowledges. In an industry that is frequently accused of excluding women, I ask Andrea if she believes female directors are any different to their male counterparts. 'In their craft? There is no difference,' Andrea says firmly. 'It's the individual, yet there is this persistent notion women are maybe too emotional, or not reliable... I don't know where that comes from. In my experience, women are just as highly skilled, professional and disciplined. So it's not gender. Yet the stats for female directors, writers and so on are shockingly low. I don't understand why that is.'

My Take on *Dear Frankie*

Running away from one's past (and thus having to confront it) is a staple feature of both spec drama screenplays and produced content, so *Dear Frankie* is no different in this regard. We join the story with Lizzie, her mother, Nell, and Lizzie's nine-year-old son, Frankie, packing up and moving again. The deaf Frankie provides a voiceover for the proceedings in the form of a letter to his father, whom he believes is a merchant seaman. Lizzie is a deeply troubled young woman who lives hand to mouth after running away from her husband, Davey, when Frankie was just a baby. Nell accompanies Lizzie wherever she goes so as to maintain a relationship with her only child and grandson, but also to 'make sure [Lizzie] never goes back'. As the narrative progresses, the reason for Lizzie's fragile mental state and Nell's concern for her daughter becomes clear: Frankie was not born deaf, but was made so by Davey, who was violent and abusive to them both. So Frankie is not writing to Davey, whom he has never met, but a PO box number. Lizzie picks up the letters and writes back to him, pretending to be a benevolent father figure who sends Frankie lively stories of life at sea and stamps for the boy's growing collection.

Many spec drama screenplays rely too much on coincidence to help fuel the plot, but *Dear Frankie* successfully uses a small contrivance to kick off the story that comes next. The movie illustrates perfectly that a coincidence *can* work in screenwriting, as long as it gets the protagonist into trouble rather than out of it. Sometimes the question isn't 'Why?' but 'Why not?' So the inciting incident in *Dear Frankie* comes not in the shape of a crisis, but a seemingly harmless embellishment Lizzie makes in one of the letters. When she buys a stamp with a picture of a ship on, she tells Frankie in the letter that it's the very ship Davey sails on. This is Lizzie's fatal mistake, however, because the ship DOES exist... and is due to dock the very next week in the town where Lizzie, Nell and Frankie now live! To make matters worse, Frankie's classmate and 'frenemy', Ricky Monroe, bets Frankie his own Top Trumps cards in exchange for Frankie's beloved stamp collection that Davey will not want to see his son. Lizzie is caught in a quandary: not only will she shatter Frankie's illusions if she confesses to having written the letters, but he will lose his precious collection and be humiliated in front of his classmates! The addition of Ricky Monroe's bet is a masterstroke in the story, because it means we totally believe Lizzie's reticence to reveal the truth to Frankie, despite Nell urging her to come clean. After all, Frankie is nine years old, the sort of age when many children discover that Father Christmas, the Tooth Fairy and the Easter Bunny are their parents' well-meaning fabrications, so it might have stretched credulity if Lizzie had carried on the story without at least considering him old enough to handle the truth. But Frankie is already the outsider on the basis of his deafness and the fact that he is the new boy, which means we do not blame her when Lizzie resolves to pay a stranger to pose as Frankie's father, just for a short visit that coming weekend. Though this is Lizzie's story, it's not Lizzie who wants to save face; she really does have Frankie's best interests at heart, so we forgive her (somewhat overbearing and ill-judged) intervention.

It would have been very easy to play *Dear Frankie* as a comedy, with Lizzie 'auditioning' various unsuitable candidates for the role of Frankie's pretend father, but it does not go down this route. Lizzie is very much lost, living solely for her child, so her journey to the pub to 'find a (random) man' is heartbreaking in its naivety. We can believe her tears and shame, sitting on the bench all night, until her friend and employer Marie finds her. Lizzie is desperate, and that's why we can believe it when Nell backs off, not interfering when Marie puts

Lizzie in touch with a man (who the script and the film simply call 'The Stranger'), despite Nell's own huge misgivings. But *Dear Frankie* is not a romance, either. No sparks fly when Lizzie and The Stranger meet in the coffee shop. The Stranger is suitably enigmatic, failing even to give his name. He is not droll or witty like we might expect, making quips about the odd situation. Lizzie is awkward and formal and we're not even sure until the last minute that The Stranger will even do it, until he says, 'What time would you like me to be there?'

So Lizzie pays The Stranger for the visit, with Frankie overjoyed when his 'dad' turns up at the football trials, as promised. We watch with glee as Ricky Monroe has to hand over his Top Trumps cards: 'You won them fair and square,' The Stranger says to Frankie. Simple boyhood pleasures are perfectly illustrated in this sequence: football; beach walks; skimming stones across the water. Again, it would have been easy for The Stranger to get this wrong and try to impress Frankie in some overblown way (or, worse, for someone else to mistake him for a potential threat to Frankie), but we get the feeling this is a man who knows how little boys tick. We are not concerned for Frankie: we realise The Stranger won't drop the ball and reveal he is not really Frankie's Dad; nor will circumstances conspire against them. Yet it's still as much a surprise for the audience as it is for Lizzie when The Stranger asks to see Frankie again, the next day. Lizzie is dubious, but The Stranger cannily asks in front of the boy, leaving her with little choice but to say yes. Lizzie finds herself being dragged along with Frankie to the docks and they all spend the day (and much of the evening) together, a faux family, pretending for Frankie's sake.

Yet it's important to note that it's not Frankie who is the protagonist of *Dear Frankie*, but Lizzie: she must learn to let go of her past and trust again – not only other people, but herself. Lizzie has spent years chastising herself for 'allowing' Frankie's father to hurt him, and the boy's deafness is a constant reminder of what she feels is her failure both as a mother and as a human being. The Stranger is instrumental in her making this important realisation, but so is the fact that Davey's sister tracks them down during the course of the narrative. Again, the expected route would have been for The Stranger and Frankie's 'real' Dad to meet and clash during the weekend, with The Stranger 'standing up' for Frankie and Lizzie. But the two men never cross paths. Instead, the sister breaks it to Lizzie that Davey is dying and wants to see his son one last time. Lizzie is unrepentant at first, saying she doesn't care, despite the sister's pleas; we don't feel Lizzie is heartless, either, since Davey's sister acknowledges the terrible wrong done to them by Davey. But because she is fundamentally a good person, Lizzie ends up going to see her ex, though she does not take Frankie with her. A fantastic sequence follows, because we feel sorry for the broken-down Davey at first, lying in bed, weak and feeble. Yet, within minutes, Davey has reverted to type, angry and calling Lizzie names, so we know she was right not to bring Frankie, as does she. Lizzie gains peace at last, not from Davey's impending death, but from the knowledge she was right to leave him, in order to protect Frankie.

Ultimately, The Stranger returns to sea and writes to Frankie for real. Revealed to be Marie's brother, we have the burgeoning hope he and Lizzie might get together in the future, though there is no proper hint of that yet. Instead, the resolution plays out a twist, both for Lizzie and for us: when Frankie writes back to The Stranger, he reveals he knows his real father died, thus telling us he knew all along it was his mother he was writing to. This could have come completely out of left field, but for three clues in the writing, painstakingly set up in the narrative:

- *Frankie's silence.* Frankie speaks just once (and to The Stranger at that) in the course of the movie. Lizzie tells her mother she keeps writing so she 'can hear his voice'. When we realise Frankie knew all along it was Lizzie he was writing to, it clicks with the audience that he wanted to talk to her as well; he was not shutting her out as Lizzie feared.

- *The PO box.* When Lizzie meets The Stranger for the first time, she says she has told Frankie that all post that goes to ships has to go through a 'centralised system' or similar, meaning he 'never questions' the PO box number. But if Frankie knew it was his mother he was writing to, he wouldn't.

- **The book.** When The Stranger arrives, he brings a present for Frankie – a book. When Frankie sees it is about his favourite subject – stamps – he signs, 'How did you know?' Both Lizzie and Nell are flummoxed at this odd question, telling him, 'From your letters, remember?' But of course Frankie is asking how The Stranger knew, because Frankie knows The Stranger isn't really his father.

Dear Frankie is a great example of a story that could easily have played out in a number of different ways, such as romance or comedy (or even both), yet the version we actually get proves the more difficult route is often the most meaningful. *Dear Frankie* is a melancholy, yet ultimately heart-warming, drama about the joys and pains of mothering.

What We Can Learn from *Dear Frankie*

Write Tips:

- Never go the 'expected' route when it comes to story or characters in your own spec drama screenplays. Yes, the expected might be easier, but the more difficult path always pays dividends.

- Recognise the importance of script development, especially script readings (with actors, if you can). Enter initiatives like the BAFTA Rocliffe New Writing Forum and/or set up your own.

- When it comes to character elements like Frankie's deafness, it's really important that this portrayal is realistic. Whilst your own budget may not allow for workshops and interpreters or similar (such as the makers of *Dear Frankie* were able to afford), it's still possible to pursue free research opportunities, especially via the internet, social media and/or Skype.

- Don't be afraid of small coincidences in plotting, like the stamp, as long as they get the protagonist INTO trouble, not out of it.

- If you want to utilise a twist at the end of your spec drama screenplay, be sure to set this up adequately, so it does not come out of nowhere, leaving the reader (and potential audience) feeling cheated.

Selling Points:

- With so much focus on female protagonists and characterisation at the moment, the pendulum has perhaps swung too far the other way, with male POVs sometimes excluded altogether from a lot of spec drama screenplays. Yet *Dear Frankie* shows a woman-centric story can still include boyhood ideals and desires, such as the need for a father figure to look up to and model oneself on. A sense of balance is key and offers more opportunities to sell the story 'off the page' to potential male collaborators, as well as audience members.

- Don't be afraid of challenging yourself and the material: it was a long time before Andrea hit upon the notion of making Frankie deaf, which undoubtedly meant a significant amount of research and rewriting. But this element broke the story 'open' and gave the story its unique selling point (USP).

- Andrea's story shows that both short films and entering schemes and competitions can be a great way of getting noticed. Discount nothing. Connect with as many people as possible and keep going with your projects. Andrea was contacted by that initial producer about Shona Auerbach because she had put herself out there.

- Like Andrea, recognise what actors can bring to your material, both in your mind's eye and/or in the finished article. They are not puppets; they can breathe life into your characters. What are you GIVING them, besides the story?

- There is certainly less development money around nowadays than ten years ago, so you may have to collaborate with producers for nothing in the first instance. Make sure you all share the same vision for the project and what you want to get out of it – you will probably spend a lot of time with these people!

COMMON WRITER AND DRAMA MISTAKES

THE AUTHOR IS DEAD?

Theme in produced drama may be subtle, or it may be delivered with force like a brick to the face! Whatever the case, one's theme or message can be ambiguous because visual imagery can mean different things to different people. This may lead to heated debates, especially online, about what certain images, stories and characters mean; and this in turn can even lead to wild speculation and insults, including libellous posts, statuses and articles in which labels such as 'racist' or 'misogynist' are applied to writers and filmmakers because their crimes are allegedly 'apparent' on screen. No. Absolutely not. We must remember a story is by its very nature fictional (even if a 'true' story!) and it is foolish in the extreme to assume a wish to tell a story automatically indicates some kind of latent desire to do someone down. If we terrorise writers and filmmakers and make them think twice about tackling difficult and controversial story matter, it won't be long before we are left with only recycled material. Since there's too much of that in the spec pile already, we do not want writers and filmmakers shying away from challenging story matter.

Continuing the idea of personal interpretation, when theme is understated it's possible for a screenwriter and filmmaker to be at odds, not only with each other regarding the story and what it means as it is rendered as image, but with their audience too! Viewers may see another theme or message, or miss the one intended entirely, when the movie is released. That said, stories are by their very nature a communication, so it's likely some, if not all, of a message will get through, even if its decoding may depend on the experiences, prior knowledge, and/or abilities of the audience. What's more, by accepting that variety is the spice of life and that there is no 'correct' way to view theme, said screenwriters and filmmakers can be treated to new, interesting and exciting ways of viewing their work by audience members. As long as both sides remember no one has the right to tell others how to view a work, no matter what the intention behind it was, what's not to like?

COMMON THEMES AND MESSAGES IN SPEC DRAMAS

As we've already established, most produced drama content features one of four major themes – morality, truth, responsibility and enlightenment – although, needless to say, there is a wide array of different subtypes of produced dramas mining those themes, to which I will return in due course. First, however, I'll put under the microscope some of the messages I see most often in spec drama screenplays:

- **Life is shit.** If you think a typical drama screenplay is one big misery fest, you're not alone: I'd bet real money that about 90 per cent of scribes attempting speculative drama screenplays think the same! As a result, the spec pile is infected – yes, infected – with a huge proportion of drama screenplays whose only message, apparently, is 'Life is shit'! In these types of spec drama screenplays, clichéd characters (crying mums, violent boyfriends, bent coppers) live in depressing surroundings (tower blocks, sinkhole estates, skanky cities), fighting familiar problems (addiction, mental health issues, domestic abuse). But even if so many writers didn't do this it would still be dull. Though a drama target audience may want to be challenged, they do still want to be entertained; it may be via a different way to, say, a movie like *Jurassic Park* (1993), but they want to be able to take away something positive, usually, from the experience. Forget that at your peril.

- **You can never escape what you are.** This notion of 'inevitability' in a spec drama screenplay is not a bad thing per se, but predictability definitely is. If a character is his or her own worst enemy, the reader (and thus the potential audience) needs to believe that the character COULD turn it around until the very last second. Similarly, a storytelling or literary device like non-linearity or dramatic irony needs to 'pay off' in the resolution that you set up earlier, otherwise your character's descent is simply dull, with them 'standing still' for most of the journey.

- **Crime pays.** Writers of spec drama screenplays who deliver the 'crime pays' theme in their work typically create characters with very jaded and bitter world views, often in the belief this makes the protagonist in particular an 'anti-hero'. It doesn't. Though the character gives the illusion of moving forward, this is usually so he can rant about the state of the world and how unfair everything is. This is not edgy. Like the previous two approaches in this list, it's just boring, I'm afraid!

- **Men destroy women.** It should be noted that male writers are just as likely to 'do' this theme as female writers. As I frequently point out on my website, I have seen NO correlation between the gender of writers and the material they create, especially nowadays: women are just as likely to write genres like science fiction or horror as men (though this was not always the case, in my experience). So writers often express surprise when I flag this theme up as being potentially a problem; surely, as an apparent 'raging feminist', I want to 'slag men off' every chance I get?? But, as I tell everyone who asks, it's patriarchy I hate, NOT men; from my POV, the theme of women's downfall being largely decided by the actions of men is patriarchal, reducing us to princesses in the tower. But even if you think that's complete hogwash – and, being theme, that's your right – I put it to you: given that 'men destroy women' is SUCH a popular theme in the spec drama screenplays pile, is it a good one to pick when we need to differentiate our stories from the hordes of others? I'm unconvinced it is. Also, of the copious numbers of drama screenplays I've read over the years with this theme or message, I've noted, interestingly, that these are the ones most likely to contain gratuitous rape scenes. A coincidence? Who knows? But one thing is for sure: nobody wants to see THAT crap.

- *Home is where the hurt is.* Growing up in an unsafe and/or invalidating environment is an unfortunate reality for so many people that it is unsurprising this message turns up so often in the spec drama screenplays pile. Again, this is not necessarily an issue, but spec drama scribes writing spec drama screenplays can make it an issue by reducing it so often to a black-and-white issue, i.e. the poor are miserable and ill-educated, with no aspirations, no parenting ability and no empathy for their partners; whereas the privileged are happy, well educated, good parents and in happy partnerships. Seriously??

MORE REASONS DRAMAS ARE A 'HARD SELL'

There is a variety of reasons why spec drama screenplays (or even just their pitches) can be a 'hard sell', but I have boiled down the main ones here:

- *Producer-led.* You may watch awards ceremonies like the BAFTAs, Oscars and Golden Globes and dream of holding one of those statuettes in your hand for your own hit drama screenplay, but you can bet your last Rolo there's a stock of producers out there thinking exactly the same thing. What's more, rather than coming up with an idea and trusting to luck, those producers are ACTIVELY pursuing that dream of theirs: doing market research; reading the trades; attending film festivals; talking to contacts; finding writers they can work with. In other words, the average writer is about fifteen thousand miles behind the average producer when it comes to this dream. So why would a producer want to make YOUR idea for a brilliant drama screenplay, when they could be making their own?

- *Adaptations.* Many produced dramas, whether award-winning or not, are adaptations of novels or plays. It's become so prevalent in fact that ceremonies have had to split many awards for screenplays into 'best adapted' and 'best original'! But don't let that fool you: it is not a level playing field by any stretch of the imagination. Getting an original drama project off the ground is supremely difficult, because it is not 'pre-sold'. A drama based on something that already exists in the public consciousness can only be a good thing, but many writers are unable to afford the huge option payments due on the most popular novels. Nine times out of ten smaller producers (never mind individual writers!) won't even get to hear about the option auctions, because the rights are sold to the highest bidder long before they're even published.

- *Permissions.* An obvious thing for a writer who cannot afford or access expensive options on popular novels and plays is to adapt something out of copyright, which in the UK is the author's lifetime plus 70 years (though this can differ country to country, so always find out exactly what the law states where you are). However, there are certain authors and playwrights out of copyright who have been mined extensively already, the most obvious being Jane Austen (particularly *Pride and Prejudice*), Lewis Carroll (particularly *Alice in Wonderland*), Charles Dickens (particularly *Oliver Twist*, but in reality all his works) and Shakespeare (again, pretty much everything!). Unless you can bring something startlingly original to these stories, it's simply not worth attempting any of these authors as a spec drama screenplay, I'm afraid. Why? Because even if you are aware of all the projects that have been produced, there are probably hundreds of unproduced ones in the spec pile already *as well*. As an example, I recall a single year in which I personally read over *20 – 20!!* – adaptations of Carroll's *Alice in Wonderland*. They varied in both quality and format – from feature, to TV pilot, to short; one was a web series – yet, strikingly, nearly all were called *Wonderland* (or similar) and followed an investigation into a girl's disappearance and/or murder in the style of David Lynch's *Twin Peaks* (1990). Extraordinary!

So, something else a writer may want to consider when tackling an adaptation for a spec drama screenplay may be a true story. The ins and outs of permissions for these are hard to nail down, with conflicting advice offered on the internet. On the true stories I have consulted on for producers, the general 'rule of thumb' appears to be:

- *'Old' history.* In the case of historical figures who lived many generations ago, it would appear scribes get a free rein, as they do with adaptations out of copyright. Even if descendants of that person are still alive, if they have no way of countering your story (especially if that historical figure is part of myth or legend) then again you should be home free (though never take anything for granted; always make sure via extensive research).

- *'Near' history.* If writing about people who are still alive, or who have died but have direct descendants still living (i.e. siblings, children, grandchildren), it is considered good etiquette to ask for permission to write the story and/or involve them in the development OR ask them to sign an option and/or legal waiver. Money may or may not change hands, dependent on the agreements made. Consulting a lawyer is a good idea in these cases: many solicitors hold free Q&A sessions 'after hours' – check the phone book and internet. But even if you have to pay for someone to draw up a letter or contract, a few hundred pounds is worth the investment, since otherwise you may waste many hundreds of hours on a story you end up being unable to use!

Obviously, in the case of both of the above, if a book about the person (fiction or non-fiction) exists, this trumps any agreement the screenwriter may be able to negotiate. That book's sole use by the writer makes the project an adaptation (even if it's a non-fiction book), on which an option MUST be paid (unless it's out of copyright). When considering permissions, then, a writer must ask whether they're worth pursuing, especially when there's money involved:

- *Investment and distribution.* Investors are basically the money men (and women) who fund filmmakers' endeavours. Sales agents and distributors are essentially the ones responsible for getting finished films into cinemas, on to DVD, streaming services and so on in all the various territories of the world. What investors and distributors want can vary and, for the last decade or so, drama has been a dirty word, with many preferring to pour their resources into projects with much higher potential returns, such as horror and comedy. This means those producers and companies with drama projects have had to find other avenues to get their films financed and made, often as 'passion projects' with no money upfront, even for themselves. Again, whilst it's not outside the realm of possibility for writers to succeed in interesting producers in their ideas for spec drama projects, it is much more likely producers will want to go with *their* own ideas if they're having to deal with the ensuing financial hardship. That's just the reality!

- *Hard to pitch!* Remember that drama concepts are by their very nature hard to pitch, so scribes often hide behind clichéd descriptions like 'Character X has to learn to live and love again', but this rarely tells your pitchee what the story IS or how they can invest in that character's journey, or why. Equally, writers often finish their pitches for spec drama screenplays with questions, such as 'Can character X manage to find himself in India, or is it too late for him?' My immediate response is always, 'Well, I dunno, can he? How would I know? You're the writer... but I'm guessing he will, else there won't be a movie!' Both times the writer has essentially made their pitch a dead end and, as a result, the producer is AGAIN not likely to go with your idea and/or pages.

- *Budgets.* Another huge problem for writers in piquing producers' interest in their spec drama screenplays is the fact that a huge proportion of writers are absolutely clueless about budgets, especially in terms of what is possible for what money when filmmaking. Too often, a writer will blithely tell a producer their drama screenplay is 'low-budget', simply because they figure it must be, as it can be shot on location and doesn't require loads of set dressing or stunts and explosions. Then the producer will come to hear the rest of the pitch or read the screenplay itself and be confronted with twenty or more speaking parts; animals; children; a stack of different locations, both interior and exterior; copyrighted material; not to mention health and safety hazards like driving, or running up and down stairs. All of these things turn a supposedly 'low-budget drama' into a medium- or even high-budget one, and just shows the producer a writer has no idea what s/he is talking about. As a result, even if you could have managed to get a read request, you've just shot yourself in the foot.

So it's all very well pitching your amazing life story as a drama screenplay to a producer, agent or filmmaker, because the likelihood they are going to think anything other than 'So?' is very small. In addition, as we know already, the average spec drama screenplay is NOT amazing. In fact, the average spec drama screenplay is barely actual drama at all, but a collection of badly realised stereotypes and tropes, thinly disguised as a story. I would even go so far as to say the spec drama screenplay is probably the WORST of all the scripts in the spec pile, which is why so many industry pros automatically shut down at the words, 'It's a drama.' Supersadface. But obviously there ARE ways of getting the movers and shakers interested in your brilliant, well-conceived, well-written spec drama screenplay. Before we look at drama niches, however, I think it's time to re-evaluate the notion of morality and theme and how different stories and imagery may mean different things to different people, as demonstrated by our fourth case study, *Kidulthood*.

CASE STUDY 4: THE MORALITY TALE

KIDULTHOOD (2006)

Written by: Noel Clarke
Directed by: Menhaj Huda
Produced by: George Isaac
Budget: £450,000

Q: What's good about it?

A: The narrative's structure is smooth and well constructed, hurtling a large cast towards the final showdown with Hollywood precision.

MY LOGLINE: After the suicide of a fellow student, a group of teenagers get the day off school. Mayhem, aggression and, ultimately, a further tragedy follow.

Writing and Selling *Kidulthood*

Screenwriter of *Kidulthood* Noel Clarke was perhaps best known as an actor when the movie came out. *Kidulthood*'s release came at the same time as Noel's breakthrough role as Mickey, Rose Tyler's boyfriend, in BBC1's flagship primetime show *Doctor Who*. I ask Clarke if he was always attached to the screenplay: 'I was supposed to play Trife but the director (Menhaj Huda) didn't want me to, as I was too old. He didn't want me to play Sam either, but I convinced him I could be intimidating if needed, and the rest is history.' I wonder if it was particularly challenging, acting in his own screenplay. Noel is quick to disagree: 'If anything, it was easier, as it was my material.' As it turns out, *Kidulthood* coming out at the same time as *Dr Who* starting again on the BBC was just a happy coincidence: Clarke tells me the screenplay was actually written in 2000/1 and shot in 2004, being in the can a good two years. So why did he write *Kidulthood*? The answer is refreshingly simple: 'I saw a play that claimed to be about the age group that I knew about and it annoyed me, so I wrote a story that I wanted to see.'

Kidulthood is renowned for supposedly having a lot of improvisation in it from the young cast, but Noel shoots this down in flames: 'There was a lot less improvisation in *Kidulthood* than people think... it was probably 95 per cent scripted.' The money for the film was raised by its producer, George Isaac, the traditional way, through his contacts. 'We had no industry help,' says Noel. When so many movies are accused of glorifying violence, I wonder if this was ever a concern for Clarke: 'There is a clear moral message in the movie – "If you behave like this, you may die, so behave." A lot of people missed the message, but that doesn't mean challenging movies should never be made; you have to make films like this.' Clarke believes the same of people's criticisms regarding race in the movie: '*Kidulthood* is not about race, it's not touched on at all,' he says. When I ask him why he thinks, then, that some people criticise the representation of young people in the movie, his answer is honest to the bone: 'People criticise everything. The things that happened in the film happen in real life. Since it's come out, I've been blamed for everything from the London Riots to the Dunblane tragedy (which actually happened in 1996, a decade before *Kidulthood* came out!)... I've literally had people tell me I'm to blame!! The truth is, society informed the film.'

Kidulthood is one of the few British movies to get its own sequel, and probably the only drama, factoring in *Bridget Jones: The Edge of Reason* (2004), *Mr Bean's Holiday* (2007), *Johnny English Reborn* (2011) and *28 Weeks Later* (2007) (and excluding the James Bonds and Harry Potters!). I ask if *Adulthood* (2008) was green-lit straight away, after the success of *Kidulthood*. As if! 'I actually tried to do other films but nobody really wanted to know about any of those, so I sat down and specced *Adulthood* because otherwise I may not have got any other film made,' Noel says wryly. Now, Noel doesn't 'just' write and act, he produces and directs too; what Americans would call a 'quadruple threat'. Screenwriting, though, is apparently Clarke's least favourite role of the four: 'If I was still just an actor, I'd starve. Writing comes from necessity.' This notion of 'necessity' really interests me, because I'm usually surrounded by those who profess to love writing and who seem frustrated by what they perceive as being the devaluing of the screenplay and what writers do by 'the industry'. In comparison, Clarke presents a scenario that's subtly different: make your own opportunities, no matter what. As he asserts: 'I've never been one to say there's a glass ceiling... if there's glass, I don't see it. If one door closes for me, I go through the window.'

My Take on *Kidulthood*

Kidulthood ultimately tells the contrasted stories of duo protagonists Trevor, aka 'Trife', and Alisa, both 15. The set-up introduces us to both of them, but also to the movie's catalyst character, Katie, a white girl who is being bullied mercilessly at school by girls in her and Alisa's class, led by the cruel and violent Shaneek: the privileged Katie sticks out like a sore thumb at the inner city school and does little to defend herself as the bullies get stuck in (we get the feeling this is a regular occurrence). Alisa is present at Katie's beating and, though she does not join in, does nothing to intervene either. We learn the reason for Alisa's reticence is because she has problems of her own: Alisa is pregnant by Trife, whom she slept with a few weeks earlier. Outside the classroom, Sam, a local hoodlum and school leaver who still wants to rule the roost, accosts Trife and friends Jay and Moony. When Sam also harangues Katie on the way out of school, it proves too much: Katie returns home and kills herself. This leads to school being cancelled the next day for all the students, so they can supposedly mourn their lost colleague. Of course, none do: instead they prepare for a party at the equally privileged Blake's house (who miraculously somehow manages to escape the same violence Katie endures).

I think there are two things that *Kidulthood* does especially well, which most drama spec screenplays generally do not, the first being structure. The set-up is extremely smooth, introducing us to the characters, their world views and their place in the movie's story world without us ever feeling that's actually what's going on. This is a rare treat in drama, especially with a large cast (too often spec screenwriters and filmmakers don't believe a reader or viewer will remember names, so introduce us to characters via the overused device of captions of their names on screen à la *Trainspotting* [1996]). Blake's party then occupies the resolution, or Act Three; thus what happens during the afternoon prior to the party provides the majority of the conflict of Act Two, which is then paid off in Act Three and leads to the death of Trife at Sam's hands.

Considering the large cast, Clarke does a brilliant job of inter-weaving all the characters' journeys together, with their paths crossing over in the course of Acts One and Two, so the party essentially becomes a showdown of epic proportions, all the characters clashing together. In doing this, the plot point of the gun is set up and paid off with Hollywood-style precision: we see Trife deliver the converted firearm to his gangster Uncle Curtis in the car in Act One, then again at Curtis's den in Act Two (when Katie's brother, Lenny, and Trife cross paths). The gun is then paid off at Blake's party in Act Three: Lenny arrives, brandishing it and threatening Sam for his part in Katie's suicide. This prompts the bleeding and mortally wounded Trife to yell, 'He's not worth it!' Of course, Sam can't keep his mouth shut and Lenny attempts to kill him anyway, only for the gun to misfire in his hand, underlining the film's strong moral message: 'Crime and violence do not pay.' The second element that I think is very well done in *Kidulthood* is the characters' journeys. As a script editor, I believe the likes of Alisa, Trife, Becky, Sam, Jay and friends are spot on within the movie's story world, for the following reasons:

- *It's* **Romeo and Juliet,** *updated.* In the great tradition of the Bard, Trife and Alisa are star-crossed lovers: circumstance, their friends, families and opposing world views will come between them, so even when they get back together at Blake's party, we just know it will end badly for them... which, of course, it does.

- **Plot message _versus_ character world view.** If the plot's message is the aforementioned 'crime and violence do not pay', the characters (unusually) reflect another world view: 'Stay true to yourself.' This is illustrated especially well by the character of Alisa, who unlike the others breaks away from the shackles of her peers' expectations and does what she thinks is right instead. Disturbed by Katie's suicide and the fact she did nothing to stop Shaneek and the bullies, for the rest of the movie Alisa starts pushing back, especially against her best friend, good-time-girl Becky. Becky places all manner of temptations in Alisa's path throughout the course of the day they're off school, to little or no avail. Though Alisa gets off to a rocky start, she rejects Becky's world view as the film progresses, the biggest flashpoint being the moment in the tube train when she yells at Shaneek in the carriage, to the onlooking Becky's abject horror. This isolates Alisa from her best friend more and more, so that by the time the party arrives that evening, she and Becky are no longer friends. Alisa, however, is unrepentant. Instead, the tear-stained and humiliated Becky finds Alisa later at the party and says: 'I'm sorry.' Alisa nods sagely: 'Yes. You are.'

  Compare Alisa then to Trife, whose own story is contrasted against his pregnant ex's throughout the film. Kicking off Act Two with a phone call to Alisa where he tells her to get lost, Trife is troubled by Katie's suicide, having had a 'thing' with her before (Katie's oblivious father mistakes Sam for Trife at the school gates). This sets Trife on the path to self-destruction that not even making up with Alisa at Blake's party can steer him away from. Though Trife doubts his place in his Uncle Curtis's gangster world and actively doesn't want to carve up the face of the guy on the snooker table, Trife is afraid – pardon the pun – of losing face himself. This scene is excruciatingly up close and personal in terms of violence, with Trife's own pain at visiting this heinous act on another human being totally visible, yet he does it anyway. Trife does not stay true to himself, unlike Alisa. As a result, just like Becky, he 'gets what he deserves', hence Trife's desperate last warning to Lenny about Sam: 'He's not worth it!'

- *Eliciting audience emotion.* Drama screenplays concerning young people frequently have characters making important realisations about their place in the world and *Kidulthood* is no exception. There is a strong sense of morality and justice to the movie, but crucially we are still gutted when Trife dies in Alisa's arms, as this lays to waste their hopes and dreams, or any chance of Trife's potential redemption. I think what's so poignant about this element of the film is that Alisa is a realist: at the party, she tells Trife they have to 'at least try' to have a relationship for the baby's sake, suggesting she means if not as lovers, then as friends. Alisa is mature and has a level head on her shoulders; we know she will essentially be alone with Trife gone, since her own mother is so unwitting and Becky has already proved she will do nothing but let Alisa down. Alisa's entire future is ripped from her and the baby, all because of a stupid vendetta between Trife and Sam. It's a tragic waste and makes us angry, but that's what good drama screenplays do: they elicit emotions in the viewer, even negative ones.

- *Gritty realism versus sensationalism?* Whilst it's certainly true *Kidulthood* takes about a year's worth of teen crises and compresses them into a single day, it's important to remember movies are a representation of 'real life' NOT real life. As Noel himself insists, these things are happening already and have been for decades; I see nothing in *Kidulthood* I have not read about in the news; heard from working with teenagers as a teacher; or experienced first-hand myself, such as underage drinking or teenage pregnancy. But, again, *Kidulthood* is not about being in a gang; it is instead a doomed love story between Trife and Alisa.

- **Story world reversal.** What's also refreshing about *Kidulthood* is the fact white people occupy the secondary and peripheral roles people of colour traditionally play in mainstream films. Instead of a predominantly white cast, with just a few PoCs, the story world is reversed. This is particularly obvious in the infamous snooker table scene. A powerful man of colour, Uncle Curtis has a white henchman holding the unfortunate guy down, in readiness for Trife to cut his face as part of his gruesome initiation into Curtis's world. In addition, though white characters like Jay and Becky may perform important role functions, neither of them occupies the same story space or drives the action like protagonists Trife and Alisa, or antagonists like Sam and Uncle Curtis.

What We Can Learn from *Kidulthood*

Write Tips:

- Noel wrote *Kidulthood* because he was annoyed with another creative work, which he felt was not truthful about the world he knew about. This can be a really great catalyst for kick-starting writing your own drama screenplay: think WHY you felt that piece had no emotional truth and how you would do it differently and why. But don't forget to research too and see if that alternative version has been done already!

- Do you have something specific you want to say? If you have a message that burns within you, chances are you will want to include a moral meaning to your story. In the case of *Kidulthood*'s message, as Noel says, it's 'Behave like this, you may die' or, rather, 'There are consequences for everything we do.' Don't forget that the inclusion of a moral message is what actively defines this subtype of drama, so don't leave your moral message to chance; develop it from the outset. All the characters in *Kidulthood* do things that relate to the message and 'get what they deserve', especially Trife (even though Alisa does go against the expectations of the group and her baby will end up fatherless, we 'know' she and the child will be okay, ultimately).

- By Noel's own declaration, *Kidulthood* is not about race, though a lot of people in the audience think it is. What we must remember as writers is that people will interpret visual images in their own way and construct their own meanings; it is not our place to tell audiences how a story is meant to be deconstructed. But by the same token, audiences have no right to impose their own vision of who writers and filmmakers are, just from the stories and the storytelling choices they make. What is right for a story may not represent that writer or filmmaker's world view and it is simplistic and foolish to decide otherwise.

- Think about the theme of your piece – what is your story about? If you don't know, no one else will either! Sometimes theme will reveal itself as you write; at other times it will emerge as you develop the project with others; sometimes it will change altogether. Be open to all possibilities, but at the same time keep in mind WHY you wanted to write this story in the first place. What excited you about it, or the characters? Knowing your own motivations will help you access your characters and therefore the theme in the long run.

Selling Points:

- In the case of *Kidulthood*, its craft was meticulous and unusual: multiple narrative threads all clash together in the resolution, with a tight, Hollywood-style structure that keeps moving forward, never letting up for a moment. This is in contrast to the majority of spec drama screenplays about young people set in deprived estates/places, which are often small affairs and very theatrical in tone, so it's not difficult to see why *Kidulthood* sold itself 'off the page' to filmmakers and investors, then ultimately to an audience.

- With morality tales come inevitable controversy. Whilst it can be unpleasant to be blamed by people for certain events that have absolutely nothing to do with one's own storytelling, that controversy nevertheless helps the film because it builds awareness, which in turn can translate to ticket and DVD sales. The phrase 'bums on seats' does not stipulate a difference between fans and haters, or even people who are neutral about a work, after all!

- Though Noel was more or less an unknown around the time *Kidulthood* was made, fast-forward two years and suddenly all that changed, thanks to his new role in *Doctor Who*. Two years after THAT, he was an Orange Rising Star Award winner! Considering he was up against the likes of Michael Fassbender at the time, this is a pretty amazing feat. Whilst a certain amount of luck was obviously involved, with all his ducks 'lining up in a row', people like Noel make things happen for themselves: he doesn't just act, he writes, produces AND directs. In other words, he realised the onus was on him and he was going to do whatever possible to get where he wanted... so he did and got it. Coincidence? I think not!

- Even though *Kidulthood* did really well, no one 'green-lit' a sequel – it was up to Noel to spec it and get it out there himself AGAIN. But this brought him even greater returns, because not only is *Adulthood* one of the few British drama sequels, he was able to direct it this time as well. So don't think you can have one success and watch the next one roll in... you won't. But if you're willing to put that work in again, you can build on your previous project and hopefully advance each time.

- Know that, sometimes, a great produced screenplay may not get distributed straight away: in *Kidulthood*'s case, it was a good two years. So keep the faith and keep going, no matter what!

KNOW YOUR DRAMA NICHE

TYPES OF PRODUCED DRAMAS

If drama is about eliciting an emotional response from the audience and asking them to appreciate a character's internal conflict, the story can basically be about anything in order to do that! Whilst we can look at stockpiles of produced content stamped 'drama', it soon becomes apparent that, although there are definite subtypes of genre such as 'cancer stories', 'stories about race', 'stories about gender', etc., this approach isn't altogether reliable. The reason for this is because, being drama, no two produced projects are even vaguely the same! It's important to note there are NO conventions or traditions to drama; no storytelling device marks them out as drama either. In addition, a produced drama may bring together multiple strands or threads from many different types of story to achieve a response in the viewer. There are quite literally no parameters at all, which is perhaps why spec drama screenplay writers find themselves lost at sea and clinging to clichés – like tower blocks, teen mums and drugs – as if they were some kind of (rapidly deflating) writing life raft! So, rather than group up produced dramas in ways that would depend entirely on the interpretation of the person doing it, I think it's far more useful to think backwards and consider what kind of emotion produced content is intending to elicit in the audience overall. As you can see in the following list, this leads to a small, but effective, selection of just six 'types' of drama screenplay:

- **Devastation.** This one is probably the most popular when writers or filmmakers think of drama screenplays, but probably not in the way we assume. Obviously the notion of 'devastation' is responsible for the plethora of nihilistic and miserable drama in the spec screenplay pile... but note I don't use that other 'D' word, 'depressing'! The difference between the two words, albeit subtle, is huge when your drama screenplay attempts to elicit emotion in the reader (and ultimately your audience). According to its dictionary definition, 'to depress' can be defined as 'to make sad or gloomy; lower in spirits; deject; dispirit; weaken; make dull'. Compare that now to 'devastating' which lists just one possibility in the dictionary: 'to lay waste'. Immediately we can see how active the latter is and how it contrasts with the weaker former word. No one may want your 'depressing drama', but that's because they want devastating drama instead! Consider the Oscar-winning greats of recent years, like *Brokeback Mountain* or *American Beauty* (1999). We are devastated, NOT depressed, by the deaths of Jack and Lester in both films. Both their deaths are a waste: Jack's because his was entirely, 100 per cent avoidable. If Ennis had just returned Jack's love, they could have been together! Jack would never have been jumped by those homophobes as he sought refuge from his overbearing family, not to mention his loneliness at Ennis's continual rejection. Lester's death is a waste because he's been such a dick for approximately 95 per cent of his life: first for letting himself 'sleepwalk' his way into a life he never truly wanted, only to 'wake' into the clichéd nightmare of a midlife crisis, the nadir of that being lusting after young girls. And then, when he realises what it is to be a man and, indeed, a human being? He dies, courtesy of his psychotic neighbour! ARGH.

TIPS: Never think you can elicit devastation in the reader of your spec drama screenplay by simply piling on the misery. *Brokeback Mountain* showed us a simple world of yesteryear in Middle America, drawing us into the period through an intriguing hook of forbidden love between two men, combined in an arena we would never have considered: gay cowboys. *American Beauty* did something quite different, mixing humour and surreal imagery with a melancholy look at failing masculinity. Both devastating endings feel completely organic: neither could have a happy ending, because that's not what the story is about. Instead, we are devastated because both characters' journeys were so inevitable, yet they were unable to swerve that resolution in time.

- **Shock and awe.** In produced content, a single character (who may or may not have existed) might guide us through these kinds of stories, which are usually thought-provoking dramas dealing with a massive issue or backdrop, such as a historical event or occurrence, like war or oppression. These dramas are frequently the 'largest' in budget and arena, so are most likely to be made by networks and studios (though often the money spent will not even equal a quarter of action-adventure budgets for summer blockbuster target audiences). Two Academy Award 'Best Pictures', nearly 30 years apart, *Platoon* (1986) and *12 Years a Slave*, were made on this basis. In the first movie, the audience is given a window into the Vietnam conflict via the eyes of Chris, a young and idealistic volunteer who learns the hard way about the horrors and barbarism of warfare; in the second, we are asked to imagine what the (real) life of talented musician and free man Solomon Northup was like when he was kidnapped and sold into slavery in the 1800s. In comparison to most produced drama which will seek to 'include' the audience on its protagonist's journey, the audience is instead much more voyeuristic in the 'shock and awe' drama, which can make for excruciating viewing as we are confronted with unpalatable truths that often really happened. Our protagonists' horror and disgust become ours as we view soldiers' rape of young women and girls they're supposed to be 'protecting'; or the beating and choking of slaves for supposed insubordination. In comparison to genre movies, however, that voyeurism may suddenly cease without warning and the audience will be pulled into the protagonist's POV suddenly and shockingly, such as when Solomon wakes, confused, in chains after dining with the two gentlemen who betray him. The message of such produced content is clear: 'Never forget', perhaps, so it might never happen again. Here's hoping...

TIPS: Shock and awe come from epic arenas and huge subject matter, not from continued mental violation. On this basis, then, whilst we may seek to corral the audience in favour of our message against injustice and tyranny, there is a very thin line between such (well-meaning) manipulation and sensationalism. Do not turn the reader off your material by being too salacious with the nastier details; often a single moment, or what we do not see, is more effective. In addition, it is important not to visually assault our intended audiences with too many locations: when considering *Platoon* or *12 Years a Slave*, our protagonists are 'anchored' in the story, both in terms of location ('the jungle' in the former; 'the master's plantation' in the latter) and time period (both are rather hazy about how much time is passing as the story goes along). It's worth remembering that being exact on the 'wheres' and 'whens' of the larger arenas serves only to confuse, not enlighten, your target audience.

- *Wonder.* These produced dramas will typically include the true story, which may be the biopic of a historical, literary or political figure, whom we may all 'wonder' about... but, crucially, it will place the audience 'behind the scenes' of that in/famous person's public life, so we might 'understand' them. Consider the biopics of two powerful women who have gone down in history, for very different reasons: *Elizabeth* (1998), a portrayal of England's so-called 'Virgin Queen'; then contrast it with *Monster* (2003), a movie based on the life of Aileen Wuornos, an American prostitute who became a serial killer. Both portrayals meant high-profile awards for the actresses portraying these larger-than-life women (a Golden Globe for Cate Blanchett as megalomaniac monarch Elizabeth; an Oscar for Charlize Theron for her interpretation of

WRITING AND SELLING DRAMA SCREENPLAYS

Wuornos's twisted world view); plus both movies did well at the box office (with the former green-lighting a 2007 sequel, *Elizabeth: The Golden Age*). Both critics and audiences alike hanker after these types of 'behind closed doors' stories, which is perhaps why 'surprise' British hit *The King's Speech* shouldn't have been that much of a surprise after all.

Yet stories that are both amazing and true are not limited to the rich and (in)famous. So-called 'ordinary people' can find themselves in the midst of events and situations that are quite remarkable, exemplified perhaps by *Erin Brockovich* (2000). The story of an unemployed single mother who becomes a legal assistant, Erin almost single-handedly takes down a California power company accused of polluting a city's water supply. *Slumdog Millionaire* (2008) is the story of a Mumbai teen who goes on the Indian version of the *Who Wants to Be a Millionaire?* quiz show and, despite being accused of cheating, goes on to win the grand prize. Again, there were multiple awards nominations and prizes given to both pictures; Julia Roberts won an Oscar for her portrayal of Erin Brockovich and *Slumdog Millionaire* swept the board at the 81st Academy Awards in 2008, with Oscars awarded for Best Director (Danny Boyle); Best Adapted Screenplay (Simon Beaufoy); Best Picture, and a host of others. It's important to note nearly all true stories – whether biopic or not – will compress time, merge characters and even completely make stuff up to tell their stories, sometimes with their subjects' support, other times without. Remember, it is neither possible nor desirable to tell the absolute truth, for it is not a documentary; thus writers and filmmakers must make difficult decisions and 'sacrifice facts for drama'.

TIPS: When it comes to biopics of the in/famous, it's very important to do one's research and discover whether those 'larger-than-life' characters have had drama screenplays written about them and/or produced content made about them before. Whilst an existing drama about the person you want to write about does not necessarily preclude your own story, it needs to be something completely new and unheard of before if you want to elicit wonder in your potential audience. In addition, many writers believe their own lives, or those of relatives, would 'make a good story', but in my experience this is rarely the case. Whilst a writer or family member may indeed have had a colourful life, this does not automatically mean it is 'enough' to sustain a drama screenplay. Again, if we are looking to cause a stir and amaze our audiences, we need to bring something new to the table to grab them. So think very carefully not only about your concept, but about the 'hook' to sell that story 'off the page'. Both *Elizabeth* and *Monster* promised audiences female protagonists we had not seen before. Though there had been many films, TV shows and documentaries about Elizabeth I, this movie offered a slightly softer, more intimate portrayal of a woman who had otherwise been portrayed as rather 'masculine' throughout history, as was necessary for the time: 'I may look like a weak and feeble woman, but I have the heart and stomach of a king!' And though audiences have been treated to many narratives involving serial killers over the years (both drama and genre, as well as true and fictional), nearly all had a male murderer at their heart. In the case of female killers, they were almost exclusively accessories, poisoners, or so-called 'Black Widows', marrying rich men and bumping them off to inherit their wealth. *Monster*, then, was immediately different from the rest by having a female serial killer who shot her victims to death, and the fact it was a true story added to its appeal. Finally, in the case of true stories about so-called 'ordinary people', what often makes them appealing is the 'triumph of the underdog': audiences want to believe that they too would stand up for themselves or do what may be deemed 'the right thing'. Erin Brockovich fits this notion exactly; she is an unlikely heroine, but that is why we love her. In contrast, *Slumdog Millionaire* has more of an 'everyman' at its heart, so instead it's more wish fulfilment for the audience: after all, who wouldn't want to win such a huge prize? As a result we root for him to prove his worth, not to mention his love for Latika in the subplot.

- **Bittersweet.** Frequently referred to as the 'anti-rom com', the bittersweet drama typically explores the notion, 'It is better to have loved and lost than to have never loved at all.' Bittersweet dramas will frequently place romances at their heart and detail relationship breakdowns or what their characters learn in the wake of the split, as in *(500) Days of Summer* or *Eternal Sunshine of the Spotless Mind* (2004). This is in direct contrast to the romantic comedy genre, which demands that the narrative convention follow a rough 'boy meets girl' (or vice versa) scenario; they hit X obstacle/s, but live 'happily ever after'. In the bittersweet drama, then, anything goes; the plot is typically looser and the characters layered, with more complicated (sometimes paradoxical) motivations for their actions. This is often reflected in a non-linear structure, often to give a direct indication of the characters' POVs as they process situations or other characters' reactions and actions, though these stories can be traditionally structured as well. Bittersweet drama does not have to include romantic relationships, however: characters may have (different) life-changing realisations based on a single moment, as in *Sliding Doors* (1998); or every member of a family may bond together and experience their own moments of self-awareness within the framework of another adventure, such as in *Little Miss Sunshine*, where this process happens via 'change agent' Olive, whom the Hoover family must get to the beauty pageant. The little girl has zero chance of winning, yet free spirit Olive just wants to have fun and inspires the individuals in her dysfunctional family to resolve their many personal issues.

TIPS: The bittersweet drama places human relationships at its heart, usually love, often utilising one character who can 'teach' the other something. In the case of bittersweet romances, the Manic Pixie Dream Girl most often teaches the Average Joe how to 'embrace life (or love)' before dumping him, as in both *Eternal Sunshine of the Spotless Mind* and *(500) Days of Summer*. When bittersweet dramas relate non-romantic scenarios, they typically revolve around the dysfunctional family instead, featuring themes like rejection, bereavement and personal ambitions. These three latter elements all feature heavily in the Oscar-winning *Little Miss Sunshine*. Rejected by his boyfriend, Frank attempts to take his own life, meaning his sister Sheryl must look after him. The whole family is screwed up thanks to the tough love of Grandpa Edwin, who now lives with Sheryl and her husband Richard, who is well meaning but nevertheless excruciatingly annoying in his steadfast belief in formulas and 'get rich quick' schemes. Their teenage son Dwayne has taken a vow of silence, ostensibly until he becomes a pilot, though in reality to 'opt out' of the general family insanity. Only Olive, the youngest member of the Hoover family, has a sensible head on her shoulders and she has much to teach all her relatives in the midst of their angst with her refreshingly simple outlook on life! So, consider your cast very carefully in your own bittersweet drama: who they are should inform what they do and what they can teach one another (and, by extension, your target audience). Beware – this also means your characters must have highly unusual motivations and outlooks themselves; for every 'usual' character trait in *Little Miss Sunshine*, such as Frank's depression at his relationship ending (typical in dramas), something highly unusual counters it, such as Dwayne's belligerent vow of silence and his resentful communication with the rest of the family via handwritten notes.

- *Hope/joy.* Often called 'dramedy', produced dramas that want to elicit the emotion 'joy' are frequently referred to as 'feel-good' and often frame this as a competition, holiday or quest. These drama screenplays may include comedic characters or plot devices and/ or thriller elements such as deadlines, with characters often having to do or find 'something' before it is 'too late'. Contests are often involved, as in *A League of Their Own* (1992), *Bend It Like Beckham* (2002) and *Fast Girls* (2012). This notion of it being 'too late' is rarely via 'life-or-death' stakes, however; it happens more on a metaphorical level, such as Shania's bad behaviour meaning she gets dumped from the team in *Fast Girls*, despite the fact the

GBR athletics relay team gets through. Shania must appeal to Lisa, the only one in the team with the power to potentially reverse the head of the team's decision, being his daughter. In doing so, BOTH girls must put their petty rivalries aside and work together, and Lisa must also realise she is running for herself, not to please her father, hence her ultimatum at the end. What's particularly refreshing about *Fast Girls* is obviously the number of female characters, as well as the unusually (sadly) large number of women of colour in primary role functions. However, in addition, for every 'usual' character (the privileged white girl; the posh, unrelenting, unreasonable dad), there is another to counteract them, such as the also posh, yet wise, physio love interest for Shania, who offers some sage words of advice that make all the difference; or the father-figure-style coach, who is nothing but encouraging, but takes no shit. The theme of *Fast Girls* is very much about second chances, so it's fitting, too, that Team GBR gets through only on a disqualification, and that Shania herself dumps the relay team at one point to concentrate on her solo running until Trix, out with an injury, insists Shania takes her place.

Perhaps most controversially for this book, however, I would argue such 'feel-good' drama screenplays ALSO include many stories couched squarely as 'family' and/or 'animation', which some believe are genres in themselves. I do not. Regarding the notion of 'family', I think films targeted at parents and their children (of any age!) fit squarely in 'hope/joy', especially given that so many carry themes and messages about growing up, getting on or family. Whilst it's true many such family movies may cross over into action-adventure territory in particular, I think it's advantageous to look at the internal conflicts of their main characters: do they have them? Pixar is a master at this, with its reliance on buddy movies such as the *Toy Story* franchise and *Monsters, Inc.* (2001), as well as its sports-orientated sequel *Monsters University* (2013). Stories designed to bring forth joy or a 'feel-good' state may also include 'coming of age' stories, which are typically live action and target older audiences, especially teens and young people, as in the case of *Juno* or *Wish You Were Here* (1987). Coming of age tales may also include the subtly different 'coming out' story, which may be positive or negative, but nearly always confusing, though characters will often be at ease with themselves and their sexuality by the resolution: examples include *My Beautiful Laundrette* (1985) and *My Summer of Love* (2004).

TIPS: It's often said by writing gurus (and screenwriting books like this one!) that 'drama is conflict', but this is often misunderstood by scribes who think automatically that conflict = TERRIBLE EVENTS in characters' lives, especially when they want to write a spec drama screenplay. This, I believe, is in part to blame for the overabundance of depressing (note: not 'devastating') drama screenplays in the spec pile, as writers attempt to pile on the misery, believing it will be 'dramatic'. It's not. It's perfectly possible to write something joyful, creating obstacles for your characters without going down the route of 'everything's ruined'. Competitive sport is by its very definition a positive arena with plenty of obstacles in the way of your characters' victories; growing up, too, though often fraught, is also a good thing, as is falling in love, yet it's also rife with emotional difficulties. So instead of automatically thinking about the negative when approaching your drama screenplay idea, consider instead a positive situation that nevertheless has many obstacles for your characters in getting what they want and need.

- *Gratitude.* Produced drama designed to elicit gratitude in its audience is frequently referred to as 'life affirming' and is most often used to relate a moral message by combining with other emotions on this list. Life-affirming stories ask us to be thankful for what we have, such as health, family, youth or happiness. Personal struggles play centre stage in this subtype of drama screenplay, especially the ubiquitous 'cancer story', but they also feature other types of illness and disability, including mental health issues and disorders such as schizophrenia, Alzheimer's, autism and strokes. Stories featuring illness and disability may be inspired by real people or true events, as in *Rain Man* (1988), a road trip drama in which a selfish yuppie must get to know his savant brother, to whom their father has left his vast fortune, or courtroom drama *Philadelphia* (1993), in which a man with AIDS files a wrongful dismissal suit when he is fired for his illness. Alternatively, they may be less loosely based on both famous and lesser-known people, though the protagonists will nearly always be 'remarkable' in some way, exceptional creatives and scientists, for example. Christy Brown was a writer and artist who had cerebral palsy and was only able to control one limb and was immortalised in *My Left Foot* (1989); *A Beautiful Mind* is the story of mathematician John Forbes Nash, Nobel Laureate in Economics, who had schizophrenia. Again, all the dramas mentioned here were nominated for, and in many cases won, multiple awards, including Oscars for such elements as writing, directing, and their stars' portrayals of the central characters.

TIPS: Illness and disability affect the lives of millions, so it's unsurprising the spec pile is full to bursting with drama screenplays about cancer and depression in particular. However, in comparison to the life-affirming dramas mentioned here, such spec dramas are often all doom and gloom, asking us to believe those characters afflicted with such conditions have wholly negative experiences. Then those sadistic writers kill the characters off at the end, making the projects seem like abject misery fests. As with what I call 'devastation drama' – which often overlaps with life-affirming drama, with good results – life-affirming drama needs to give the reader (and thus its target audience) a REASON to get on board with its lead character's journey, otherwise it just ends up depressing (and dull!). In the case of *Rain Man* and *Philadelphia*, both are stories of redemption: Charlie is presented with the autistic Raymond by his late father and essentially told that, if he wants his share of the inheritance, he has to look after him. Charlie, played to perfection by a young Tom Cruise, is greedy and selfish and takes Raymond on solely for the bucks (just as his father knew he would), but in doing so Charlie finally learns what family and integrity are about. In *Philadelphia*, a grave injustice has been done to Beckett by his law firm, yet only homophobe lawyer Miller will represent him, even though he doesn't really want to. Like Charlie, Miller is forced to revise his opinion over the course of the story. In comparison, stories like *A Beautiful Mind* and *My Left Foot*, though they will dip into emotion number one, 'devastation', are more likely to combine their stories with storytelling emotion number three, 'wonder': these are incredible people, with incredible stories 'behind closed doors'. Sometimes dubbed 'inspiration porn' (especially by disabled audience members and their families), it is important to remember that media imagery isn't received passively and that different stories mean different things to different people. Also, arguably, there is sometimes a trade-off to be had in terms of increasing awareness of a certain condition.

So, with these six (very) broad subtypes of produced drama that nevertheless have a wide variety of stories and characters driving them and relating to one another within them, what is the problem with many spec drama screenplays and the marketplace?

CASE STUDY 5: THE PORTMANTEAU STORY

NIGHT PEOPLE (2005)

Written by: Adrian Mead, Jack Dickson
Directed by: Adrian Mead
Produced by: Clare Kerr
Budget: £300,000

Q: What's good about it?

A: It twists our expectations in terms of both story and character, plus it takes in a whole city at night, but remains manageable in terms of production.

MY LOGLINE: Over the course of one night, a selection of people must make decisions that change their lives forever.

Writing and Selling *Night People*

The Scottish BAFTA-winning *Night People* is a low-budget feature with a difference: it is also a portmanteau film. The word 'portmanteau' literally means 'large suitcase'. This word first lent its meaning to the notion of 'portmanteau words', for which the writer Lewis Carroll was famous, creating many, such as 'chortle' (a combination of 'chuckle' and 'snort') and 'slithy' ('slimy' and 'lithe'). The English language now boasts a vast array of such spliced words (media-relevant words being 'blog', 'malware' and 'camcorder', to name but a few). However, the word itself also lends itself to filmmaking, for a 'portmanteau film' is basically a selection of short films linked together by a common theme to create a feature-length movie. In the case of *Night People*, the film takes place in Edinburgh, one Halloween night, between dusk and dawn.

The thematic question that links all the characters' stories in *Night People* is, 'What happens when you're on the point of change?' Its director and co-writer Adrian Mead explains further: 'People defy logic. We all have madness in us. I wanted to explore that.' From this deceptively simple beginning come five very different characters and world views:

- *Jane's story.* Jane is a driver for a drug dealer, masquerading as a taxi driver but in reality ferrying her boss around and doing his errands. On this particular night, Jane is forced to take her five-year-old daughter, Alison, out with her when the babysitter cancels at the last minute.

- *Father Matthew's story.* Originally from Madagascar, Father Matthew is disillusioned about his abilities and plans on leaving the church to go home. When the HIV-positive Mary, 15, mistakes him for a fellow homeless person, Matthew sees an opportunity to make one last difference to a member of his congregation.

- **Stewart's story.** Desperate for cash, newly single dad Stewart steals an expensive pedigree Chow dog, with the intention of selling it, much to the chagrin of his eldest child, Kelly, aged 12, and delight of his young son, Bradley, 8, who thinks the canine is his birthday present.

- **Josh's story.** Rent boy Josh, 15, frequents Edinburgh's bus station, turning tricks in the toilets to survive. When he spots young runaway David, 13, waiting for a bus, Josh makes a phone call, keeping the younger boy company until whomever he called gets there to take him.

- **William's story.** A blind man and his guide dog start out at night on an odyssey to Edinburgh's bridge, aiming to get there by dawn.

Adrian Mead tells me *Night People* was written with a very specific brief and budget in mind, for an initiative set up by the lottery-funded Scottish Screen (now Creative Scotland) and STV. Adrian was a bouncer for 17 years and started on the door of nightclubs at the tender age of 15, but *Night People* is not an autobiography, nor are any of the story threads 'his' story, or anyone else's on the production. 'I knew what [Edinburgh] was like at night; I saw a kind of different world and that always intrigued me,' Adrian says. 'This is what "write what you know" means... It's often misunderstood. Perhaps it's better to say "write from real life"? Start with something you've seen or found interesting, that has relevance to you... then expand on that.' A £300,000 budget may seem like a lot of money to an unproduced spec screenwriter – and certainly it is for a first-time feature-film director – but it doesn't stretch far for a project as ambitious as this. 'I could've done a one-room thing, like everybody else,' Adrian says simply, 'but I didn't want to. I wanted to do something cinematic. Something adventurous, yet manageable.'

This notion of 'manageability' is key in the success of *Night People* winning that grant money and getting 'off the page' into production. *Night People* feels as if it takes in the whole of Edinburgh with its panoramic shots of the city and epic landmarks, not to mention wildlife by roadsides and in the night skies, all brought in especially by animal wranglers. But, in reality, it was shot in a very small area. Adrian expounds: 'I think other people were more scared by the project than we were! We knew what we were doing.' Both Adrian and his producing partner Clare Kerr have lived in Edinburgh for years and know how to showcase their city with minimum input, for maximum output: 'Lots of those exterior locations... they were just down the road from one another. Most of the interiors, they were in the same building, or were even the same place, just dressed differently.'

When pressed for the story that caused the filmmaking team the most difficulty, Adrian insists it's the actual physical movement of the production as a whole that causes logistical headaches: 'Just getting around the place, setting up, setting down, feeding the crew and so on,' he says, though he goes on to describe the bus station scenes as being the most expensive in terms of time and money, because they had to decorate it. 'It's actually a car showroom,' Adrian laughs. 'It had just closed down a few days before. The day after we finished shooting there, the bulldozers arrived. No chance for pick-ups!' (For the uninitiated, 'pick-ups' are those shots commonly required after shooting, to clarify the story in the edit.) So what else is important in ensuring everything gets done on a low-budget production, if it's often about getting the shot no matter what? 'Over prepare,' Adrian says, without hesitation. 'And don't get too precious about the screenplay... you have to remember it's always about compromise when you start shooting.'

My Take on *Night People*

In a sea of low-budget drama screenplays and movies set in urban areas, *Night People* is a rare beast in that it reflects none of the 'usual' characters and/or scenarios the jaded script reader or moviegoer has come to expect from this type of movie. Though the story world takes in classic drama territory with the seedy side of life, such as drugs, Edinburgh looks fantastic: nowhere to be seen is the Ken Loach-style sinkhole estate, nor a single wannabe gangster, gun or stabbing. Stewart, the father in the story, might be hopeless, but he's trying and, at the end of the day, is the one who stayed, unlike the children's errant mother. Josh, the sex worker of the narrative, is male – an unusual thing in itself. Whilst we assume, just as Jane does, that William the blind man wants to reach the bridge before dawn so he might throw himself off it – suicide being a not uncommon occurrence in both drama screenplays and produced content – his real reason, despite being less melodramatic, turns out to be all the more powerful. Matthew, the priest losing his faith, is neither middle-aged, nor white, nor even British; plus his flaw is neither an illicit love for a woman, nor a sinister lust for children, which is what we might have expected. In contrast, the younger, white runaway, Mary, is the one who is HIV-positive, yet neither she nor Matthew talk of the virus's origins in Africa, or even race in general, but the universal fear that binds probably 90 per cent of all human beings (and certainly runs through all the *Night People* characters' world views): letting down the people who love us.

There were two stories that stuck out for me, ultimately. The first, unsurprisingly, is Jane's story: I say 'unsurprisingly' because Jane probably occupies the most 'story space' of all the characters in *Night People*. In addition, her story collides with that of the blind man, William: when he mistakes her for a real taxi, she ends up ignoring her drug dealer boss, Mal, on the radio and takes William and his dog to the bridge (where she also acts as the voice of the audience, pleading with him not to jump, to William's bemusement). Put simply, *Night People* begins and ends with Jane and Alison's journey, both literal and metaphorical: Jane is a victim of circumstance, both in terms of having to take Alison with her that night, but also of life: she has already had to go to prison for Mal, who, reading between the lines, may also be Alison's (unwilling and/or unwitting) father. Mal has moved on to pastures new and his present girlfriend, the beautiful Lizzy, has taken Janey's place. Demoted to driver, Jane is doing what she has to: nothing more, nothing less. So, in a bid to distract Alison and keep her occupied as she runs errands, Jane pretends their journey is a fairy story, with the various occupants of the taxi performing roles such as the ironic 'Prince Charming' – Mal – and the 'treasure' being the lockbox full of dirty money. The drugs – 'pharmaceutical grade cocaine' no less – is referred to as 'fairy dust'.

The little girl is enthralled with her mother's tale and behaves well; what's more, this never changes and Alison never once blames her mother for anything, even when referring to the time Jane had to go away to the 'evil wizard's castle' (prison). One of the most poignant moments is when Alison asks her mother if she was tortured at the castle. Eyes full of tears, Jane says she was and that being kept away from her 'wee girl' was the worst torture imaginable. In short, we can empathise with Jane, even though we may not agree with the life choices that have led her to that night. We can also sense Jane is at a crossroads in her life, so when the catalyst occurs and Alison gets hold of a packet of cocaine, we expect the little girl to ingest it and overdose. But, again, *Night People* confounds us, because the child puts it in her pocket instead. It's only later on in the night, as Janey struggles to change a tyre, that Alison gets out of the vehicle and starts laughing, throwing the 'fairy dust' into the air. Jane – and we, the audience – appreciate the true horror of not only what we're seeing, but what *could* have just happened. Even though Alison is unscathed, it's this act that tips the balance: Jane will never return to Mal. She and her child take the money and run, literally, never to return.

Like Jane's story, Josh the rent boy's contains both light and shade. This thread was ultimately my favourite of the entire movie (and Adrian's too, apparently), for three reasons:

- **Again, it plays with our expectations.** I've read so many drama screenplays (short, feature-length AND portmanteau) that include sex workers over the years that when I saw *Night People* included one AND that he was cosying up to a 'younger model', David, I will admit to rolling my eyes a little bit. I figured I had this story down, in advance: Josh would offer to take the youngster with him, effectively sell him into slavery, then pocket the proceeds, perhaps even using the money to get on a bus himself, leaving

Edinburgh to start a new life. I figured I was looking at a story about the unpalatable things we may do to survive, which is a common occurrence in gritty, realistic drama. So even though Josh saves David from that first punter, we figure it's just so he can 'groom' the young boy himself... and, throughout this narrative, as Josh continues to use the phone, urging the person at the other end to hurry up, we figure it is his pimp, who will arrive and spirit David off. Except, of course, it isn't: it's a social worker. Josh sends David off with her, effectively saving him from the life he has had to endure. Or, you can look at it another way: 'The cynical reading is, he's getting rid of the competition,' Adrian points out. 'Josh is getting older. He needs David off his patch.' Regardless of which version you personally prefer, however, that notion of playing with audience expectation is what is most powerful about Josh's story.

- *It's believable... and funny.* Josh is streetwise and street smart, watching proceedings like a hawk. Though he never exchanges a word with his punters, just a glance, we know exactly what is going on in the toilets he keeps ducking into with them... we don't need the gory details and it's more effective without them. In contrast, runaway David is completely oblivious, unaware he's being cruised by the various predatory men congregating in the station. Like Josh, David smokes but, unlike the older boy, the cigarettes dangle from his small hands and he can't light them properly, giving one such punter an 'excuse' to approach him. What's more, though this thread is obviously not funny per se, it still contains light relief, such as when Josh chastises David with, 'You shouldnae be smokin' at yer age!' in a very paternalistic manner, hinting at what comes next in the resolution of his story.

- *It's ultimately devastating.* David's arc ends happily and he leaves with the social worker, giving Josh his treasured football boots in gratitude. We leave Josh clutching the box, a smile on his face... but *Night People* does not give us time to bask in this triumph. Almost immediately, another punter approaches, giving Josh 'The

Look'. For a moment, Josh hesitates and we hope he will turn around and walk the other way, leaving his life as a sex worker behind him. But he does not. Josh not only follows the punter into the toilets, he throws the boots into an early morning cleaner's cart as he passes. This underlines that, unlike David, Josh is lost... and because we know he remembers himself 'before' (hence calling the social worker, for David), it's all the more agonising. 'I had to fight for that last shot,' Adrian says. 'Execs didn't want it. They said it was too much of a downer. But for me it was important: I wanted something devastating that would stay with you.' And it certainly does that!

I read relatively few spec drama screenplays that are portmanteaus and am always surprised at this, especially considering I read so many short films, by the same writers, who frequently mine the same types of themes and messages. It strikes me these scribes could benefit from constructing a portmanteau in the style of *Night People*, if not to produce themselves, then as an exercise on how to create a feature-length project, or as a sample to send out to agents and producers (or both!). As I am always at pains to point out on my B2W website, there is a veritable dearth of good feature-length projects in the spec pile just in general, plus TV people *will* read features, whereas film people won't always read TV pilots, or shorts on their own. Seems like a massive missed opportunity!

What We Can Learn from *Night People*

Write Tips:

- Writing with a very specific brief in mind like the one Adrian had (even one you set yourself) can 'focus' one's mind to 'real-world' constraints in terms of production logistics. Portmanteau movies can also enable spec screenwriters and filmmakers to tell dramatic stories on the 'minutiae of life' that it may not be possible to undertake over 90 minutes on their own. Just don't forget that all the 'short films' must be linked somehow by a theme, question, message and/or moral.

- Portmanteau films can work as excellent sample screenplays for selling yourself to industry contacts, as they typically incorporate complex themes, ideas and characters. You also potentially have five or six short films to submit on their own to schemes and opportunities, two avenues for the price of one!

- If you want to make your portmanteau yourself, use your real-world knowledge to inspire your story, not the other way around. Adrian and Clare set *Night People* in a small part of Edinburgh because it was a location they were very familiar with. Don't bite off more than you can chew. You can do a lot with a little.

- When selling your portmanteau film 'off the page' as a sample or as a finished movie to audiences, learn a lesson from *Night People* and be aware you need some comic relief. If ALL your stories are a complete downer, you will simply turn potential readers and viewers off your screenplay and/or film.

Selling Points:

- Realise what you can achieve with what money. Do not simply guess and hope for the best. (What's more, don't forget you need to know this BEFORE you write even a single word of the screenplay.)

- If you are a spec screenwriter or filmmaker with a day job, a portmanteau film can offer a very real opportunity to both write and make a movie in the limited time you have available. If self-financing and shooting a portmanteau movie yourself, it's possible to create each 'short film' of your portmanteau at different times, with different crews, actors and post-production teams, over the course of several months or even years, when money and opportunity allow. Just beware of losing sight of that all-important link between them!

- There are lots of ways of attempting portmanteau movies, and thinking beyond the 'traditional' methods of filmmaking can be inspiring, groundbreaking and career advancing. Adrian and his team may have made *Night People* themselves, but what if they had decided to make just ONE of the short films, set in Edinburgh... and then thrown down the gauntlet to other teams in other cities, all around the world, so that *Night People* had stories from London, Paris, Berlin, Milan, New York, Rome, Sydney and so on? It's possible to collaborate now with people you've never even met, thanks to Skype and the internet, as demonstrated by the record-breaking *50 Kisses* (2014). This movie was crowdsourced from around the globe by Chris Jones and the team behind the London Screenwriters' Festival and included drama short films, as well as genre. Though *50 Kisses* was a massive project and undertaking, there's absolutely no reason why screenwriters and filmmakers can't do this on a smaller scale, collaborating via the internet before linking their short films into one portmanteau movie.

- Clever editing can turn your portmanteau's stories into 'themed threads' within your feature-length movie, rather than a selection of shorts that have simply been cut and showcased together. Recognise, too, that there are advantages and disadvantages to both methods of approaching a portmanteau... and that there are ways of doing it no one has ever seen before, if you put your mind to it.

BEATING THE ODDS

SAME-OLD, SAME-OLD

The odds are always against any spec screenwriter, but we've established they are especially hard on the spec drama screenplay writer. People in the industry simply don't believe us when we say we're great writers with a great drama screenplay concept (although they might when we say we have a great comedy, horror or thriller to pitch). It's not that they don't want to take a punt on a great drama screenplay either; it's that they have been disappointed, not just tens, nor hundreds, but literally THOUSANDS of times by spec drama screenplays in the following two ways:

- *Samey stories.* It may be hard to believe, but every script reader or editor, producer or filmmaker has read the same spec drama screenplay, with the same story, by multiple writers in the course of their career. That samey story goes like this: 'A miserable character leads a miserable life then DIES (or life gets better *for some reason*).' Now, of course, this story CAN work (*American Beauty*, anyone??) but the familiarity with which this story turns up in the spec pile is matched only by the familiarity of its arena (or story world), which typically will be the same as well! In the case of UK spec drama screenplays, we're talking a working-class environment of sinkhole estates, tower blocks, poverty, teenage mums, drug dealer boyfriends, bad parents, bent coppers and dodgy pub landlords. US spec drama screenplays will be set in trailer parks or 'the projects' and 7-Eleven supermarkets; gangs of youths – especially people of colour – will frequent car parks ('parking lots'), buying and selling bodies and drugs out of seedy bars for the small-time Mafiosi who 'run this town'. Instances of domestic violence, addiction and rape are common in these scripts and, though the protagonist may attempt to get more from his or her life, nine times out of ten s/he will FAIL dismally, suggesting perhaps that the average spec drama writer believes it's not possible to change who or what you are.

• *Samey characters.* Somewhat inevitably, then, if the same stories happen, the same characters turn up again and again as well. What's more, they'll have the same sorts of motivations and even do the same sorts of actions! As a result, readers end up in 'tick-the-box' screenwriting HELL.

So, is it any wonder industry pros DON'T want to read our specs and go into automatic shutdown when we say, 'It's a drama'??

TYPES OF CHARACTERS IN SPEC DRAMAS

Whilst we may be confident OUR drama spec is the exception to the rest, that producer, agent or script editor you want to read it simply thinks you're yet another deluded writer with a patchwork mess of movies that already exist, with characters they see so much of that their brains may explode if they encounter yet another one. Think I'm exaggerating? Let's look at the characters I see most often in drama screenplays in the spec pile.

MALE

Due to the samey stories and arenas, male characters in spec drama screenplays have limited role functions, being typically defined by violence, abuse and addiction, though some attention may be given to their jobs, or relationships. Interestingly, crime is an overriding element of many spec drama screenplays, meaning gangsters and cops feature heavily; as does being 'clever' and what that means (especially the dichotomy of 'book smart vs street smart', and especially when it comes to the chemistry student who can mix and sell drugs!). Check these out:

- **Tortured Hero.** Tortured Hero has ISSUES, which is not really surprising, considering his wife and family are usually dead (or have at least left him). Cast into a society that measures men by their jobs and what they can provide for others financially, Tortured Hero typically is bitter and must learn 'how to live again'. Sometimes spec drama screenwriters attempt to write a Tortured Heroine in the same vein who must realise materialism or the beauty industry will chew her up and spit her out in the same way. Whatever the case, both versions of this very familiar character will have to realise their souls are as hollow as a chocolate Easter egg and they're slowly melting under the pressure of MODERN LIFE. As drama screenplay premises go, this isn't a terrible start, but has been done rather a lot, and to make it float your characters need to have 'left of the middle' motivations or realisations to make, otherwise they will read as 'same-old, same-old', which is precisely what you don't want in an already crowded marketplace.

- **Good Guy Gangster.** This protagonist may be an actual gangster, or forced to act like one: usually meeting violence with violence (most often to protect a woman and her child). The Good Guy Gangster will feel compelled to 'save' those who are vulnerable, usually because his own family was murdered or died in an accident that was his fault, either directly or indirectly. Good Guy Gangster is often a former soldier, who has fallen on bad times financially and/or emotionally, to account for his hermit-style life and his killing skills. He will also be fighting suicidal thoughts and, to 'prove' he's not a two-dimensional hard case, will visit the graves of his dead family and cry a lot.

- *Bad Guy Gangster.* The antithesis of Good Guy Gangster, he will turn up most frequently as the antagonist in those stories, though he is sometimes the protagonist of his own. In the former, he will obviously pose the threat to the woman (and/or her child), and his position in the community may vary: he may be a Mafioso or drug dealer, or he may be her (dodgy) boss, especially in a seedy pub or club. He will typically be a rapist as well as ruthless. In the latter, Bad Guy Gangster will grow weary of killing and want a new life, as represented by the woman of the storyline, but will be unable to achieve this, as he will be drawn back into bloodshed, typically getting killed in the process.

- *Gangster in Training.* Usually a teenager or in his very early twenties, Gangster in Training generally comes from a deprived background and has started off his life of crime as a petty thief or dealer for small-time crooks, in stolen goods or cars, or drugs. From there he will get 'head hunted' by Bad Guy Gangster and asked to prove his loyalty and his worth to BGG's organisation, doing more and more reprehensible things. Gangster in Training may enjoy his descent into depravity, or he may feel he has no choice: often he has a 'softer side', looking after an invalid relative or much younger siblings. Frequently he will be forced to inform on BGG by a cop character, who is an Idealist (next).

- *Idealist.* Idealist will be young and book smart; he has strong opinions, is probably college or university educated and probably ill-equipped for the realities of life on 'the street'. Despite this, he will learn over the course of the narrative to trust his instincts and will usually be left standing at the end of the story. He provides an obvious contrast in narratives with an Old Timer character (next).

- *Old Timer.* An Old Timer will be a veteran of life and/or a job and, typically, is paired up with the Idealist. Old Timer is street smart and usually grouchy and out of shape. He relies on gut instinct, yet despite this will frequently get killed in the story; and, when he doesn't, he's often Behind It All, especially if there is blackmail or loot involved: he needs it, for his retirement/wife with dementia's care/disabled daughter when he's gone, etc.

- **Angry Young Man.** The Angry Young Man is often entitled and feels life has let him down in some way. He will have a poor-paying job or little direction in life, though he will often have a talent, most commonly sport, music or drawing. Often he will require the services of a Mentor to turn his life around (next).

- **Mentor.** A Mentor character will often guide the Angry Young Man, though sometimes the Idealist as well. Mentors are often Old Timers, though they don't have to be; in the best spec drama screenplays Mentors don't 'know everything' and will have their own arcs as well.

- **Bad Dad.** Most commonly from a working-class background, Bad Dad will be an alcoholic, a gambler, violent, ill-educated and/or a sexual abuser of his children. He will most often be out of work and view his family as his possessions. Power is everything to him, but once our protagonist finally stands up to him and realises how pathetic he is, he will be crushed fairly easily, committing suicide or even handing himself in to the police.

- **Dead Dad.** Most commonly from a middle-class or privileged background, Dead Dad will appear most often in flashbacks. Unlike Bad Dad, Dead Dad will be a fantastic father but his loss early in the protagonist's life will create a void s/he can never truly fill (and it usually is a female character, FYI).

- **Best Friend/Henchman.** A sounding board for the protagonist, or a literal dispenser of hard justice for the antagonist, the Best Friend or Henchman is frequently a two-dimensional character in the spec pile. This is a shame, because some of the best secondaries in produced drama have performed these role functions, but they need their own personalities and motivations to really work.

FEMALE

Produced drama screenplays feature female protagonists almost as often as male, and spec drama screenplays are no different in this regard. However, scratch the surface and it is immediately apparent female characters appearing in spec drama scripts are too often defined by their role as a parent, or their sexuality (or both). Check these out:

- *Numb Mum.* Often in the place of the Bad Dad or Dead Dad characters, Numb Mum will be present in the narrative, orbiting our (usually, young) protagonist. If she has a working-class background, she may struggle with depression and stay in bed all day, crying or staring into space; in other scripts she will be an alcoholic, bringing strangers back for sex, despite small children in the house. If she has a middle-class background, she will care little for her children's emotional welfare, preferring instead to kit them out with the latest gadgets and designer labels, believing material goods and 'keeping up with the Joneses' are what it takes to be a good mother.

- *Oblivious Wife/Mother.* The Oblivious Wife/Mother is as her title suggests: she's so focused on herself and her own problems, she hasn't a clue what's really going on under her nose. Oblivious Wives/Mothers from middle-class backgrounds will concentrate on their jobs to the detriment of their children, not noticing they are being bullied in school (and, more recently, online via social media), which will often lead to a young character's suicide. If from a working-class background, Oblivious Wife/Mother will not notice her husband sexually abusing one or all of the children in the house, or will turn a blind eye and make excuses for his violence towards them and/or her.

- *Teen Mum.* Teen Mum turns up in many spec drama screenplays and nearly always in the negative: too often she is stupid and/

or 'slutty', suggesting she 'deserves all she gets' (most often violence, especially rape). Even when Teen Mum is portrayed as smart, the overriding message from many spec drama screenplays is this character is now 'doomed' to failure and caught in the poverty trap forever (as is her child, presumably). As a teen mother myself, this is a particular soapbox of mine: I have met many smart and educated young mothers who've worked their way out of poverty and this continuous cycle of negative portrayals of teen mums seems utterly bizarre to me.

- *Jealous Mum.* Often a Teen Mum herself once, Jealous Mum is now in her late thirties or early forties and the so-called 'bloom of youth' has left her, which she bitterly resents. As a result, she and her daughter will be at each other's throats, with Jealous Mum conspicuously in the wrong nine times out of ten, suggesting in many spec dramas it's only looks that 'make' a woman! YIKES.

- *Sassy Friend.* Frequently written as a role for the only woman of colour in the screenplay (since her race will be noted, whilst no one else's is, indicating that they 'must' be white?), the Sassy Friend knows how life works and fulfils a kind of Mentor function for the protagonist. This in itself wouldn't be a major issue if it weren't for the fact that Sassy Friend's 'blackness' too often marks her out as being obese and hilarious (seriously?). Now, that's not to say larger women of colour shouldn't be part of a narrative; of course they should – this is drama, we can write ANYTHING and, frankly, all writers should be thinking of ways to include marginalised voices wherever they can as far as I'm concerned. But too often Sassy Friend ends up as a kind of glove puppet for what the audience is thought to want, which is 'steering' the protagonist into nonsensical situations. But this is not what we want. We want characters with depth, whom we can relate to!

- *Bitch.* Sometimes a Temptress/Moll (next), the Bitch is commonly a cop, wife, mother-in-law or best friend. She epitomises the notion 'with friends like these, who needs enemies?' which could be great for potential conflict if her methods in spec drama features were not so obviously catty, making us wonder why the protagonist puts up with her and ultimately impacting on the reader's suspension of disbelief. Also, the Bitch usually does little to push the story forward, being present only to say Bitchy lines.

- *Temptress/Moll.* Often the girlfriend of Bad Guy Gangster, she may seduce Good Guy Gangster, either falling for him for real or as a honey trap. All tits and ass, she flaunts her sexuality and uses it as a weapon, but is usually more caricature than character.

CHILD

- *Little Lolita.* Usually under 17, but not younger than 13, Little Lolita has become aware of her developing body and uses it to get what she wants from much older men. Frequently an orphan and/or runaway, she's smart and older than her years, often already 'tainted' by the streets and/or her situation, which forces her to do what she does, even if she does not actually have sex. If she is from a privileged background, she will have been raised by a succession of nannies, rarely feeling the love of her parents, an orphan in all but name. She is cynical, lost and unaware of the concept of 'normal' childhood.

- *Precocious Child.* Bright and full of life, the world holds many wonders for Precocious Child, who has a few things to teach the adults in the narrative. Often the child will have a special talent, skill and/or disability, so the adult in the story must access the Precocious Child's world view via other means and, in doing so, learn what is 'important'.

- *Bully.* Bullies are nearly always present in a spec drama narrative when there is a child protagonist, and since nearly everyone gets bullied at school, the Bully could be a good character, especially if the reasons for why s/he is the way s/he is are explored. However, this is hardly ever the case and the Bully is too often a two-dimensional stereotype in the spec drama screenplay.

STEREOTYPE VERSUS ARCHETYPE

The problem many writers have when it comes to characterisation, especially in drama screenplays, is they confuse stereotype with archetype: the difference is subtle, but huge. Stereotypes are perceived negatively, because they are oversimplifications of what people 'are'. If you take a moment to consider 'real life' and apply certain stereotypes to yourself, immediately you can see the problem. For example, I live in Devon in the UK, yet none of the stereotypes associated with living in a rural area – second homes, lots of money, farming, lack of education, blood sports! – apply to me. Not one. And this is why people get angry when they see characters stereotyped on screen, since they immediately feel it is an unjustified slight on themselves and/or others.

In comparison, then, an archetype is altogether different from a stereotype. Originating from the Greek 'arkhetupon', meaning 'something moulded first as a model', its meaning is clearly much more positive from the offset when considering the operative word in the definition is 'first'. We're not recycling old prejudices and assumptions via stereotypes; we are CREATING new ways of looking at characters. How can that be anything but a good thing? In other words, you need to take a character and put your own unique and authentic twist on him or her, instead of simply shoving a character we've already seen loads of times before into your work. This aspect is non-negotiable if you want readers (and thus filmmakers, not to mention audiences) to get on board with your spec drama screenplay.

So, with the list of spec characters from the last section in mind, I would ask: where's the Manic Pixie Dream Girl archetype? Or the Everyman (or Woman!)? Or the spoilt brat? Or the Lost Boy or Girl, who doesn't have to be literally lost, but lost emotionally? Or the

'Rock Star', who doesn't have to be an actual rock star, but thinks everything is about him or her (usually him)? Or the change agents, who change very little themselves, but end up changing all the secondary characters in some way? Excepting a few, most in the list are okay as starting points, but you have to add to them. The point of drawing writers' attention to the 'usual' characters in the spec pile is not to say they're all crap and you should completely start again. We don't want to go from one end of the scale to the other; you don't have to reinvent the wheel. Instead, figure out who your characters are, what they want and why we should get on board with them by working out what is the 'same but different' about them, as producers always say? We want something we can recognise, yet have never seen before, that's all (!).

THERE IS NO 'RIGHT' WAY TO TELL A STORY

Though there is more writing and filmmaking information freely available 24/7 to writers and filmmakers now than at any point in history, it has come at a price. Rather than use this information as a springboard for ideas about what works when it comes to storytelling, many writers and filmmakers pour their efforts into discovering the 'right way' to tell a story. NEWSFLASH: there is NO right way to tell a story out there and, even if there was, I wouldn't want to pay attention to it. The key to good storytelling is in one's own gut. Anyone who tells you otherwise is at best a div and at worst lying to you so they can part you from your hard-earned cash. There is no 'right way', only YOUR way. However, it is also important to remember NO ONE (not even an Oscar-winning screenwriter!) knows how to tell a great story through intuition alone. If you want to be sure the story for your spec drama screenplay really is great, I would recommend asking yourself the following BEFORE you spend X amount of hours writing it:

- *What is my concept?* Always write an initial logline. That doesn't mean you need to marry it; you can swap it later. Just remember that if you can't write a logline, you'll run into trouble with the screenplay! Doh.

- **Does it work?** Some writers like to hold their concepts to their chest like jealous kids, sure their ideas are SO AMAZING other people will steal them at a moment's notice; other writers are simply embarrassed, either because they sense their ideas are underdeveloped, or because they don't like asking for help (sometimes both). Most writers are somewhere in-between these two extremes. But trust me when I say you NEED to ensure your concept works... so DO tell it to other people whenever you can. It doesn't have to be other writers if you don't want; the simple act of talking your concept through with friends, your partner, your dog (!), will MAKE you concentrate on it and ensure it's not holier and stinkier than that old, mouldy, forgotten sock under the bed.

- **What has gone before?** Identify the threats, such as those stories that are VERY like the concept you want to write, and again think about what's different in yours. Don't forget to also identify the opportunities, not only in terms of produced projects, but potential target audiences. In addition, if you are unable to find produced content dealing with your subject matter, when it comes to drama this can often be a VERY good thing!

- **Who are the characters?** Characterisation is important in all screenwriting, obviously, but arguably it's most important in drama screenplays because they are 'character-led', via that notion of 'internal conflict'. This does not mean all your characters have to be 'likeable', but equally it doesn't mean you'll be able to get away with your characters being total shits either. Great drama screenplays know that people are not black and white, so protagonists may not be 'good' and antagonists may not be 'bad', but they will all be relatable.

- **What is learned in the story?** If you recall, most drama screenplays place an overt message or theme at the heart of the story and frequently characters will learn something in order to communicate that to the target audience. I call these 'transformative arcs', which are frequently demonstrated by the 'coming out' and/or 'coming of age' tale. But this isn't the only reason I chose *Beautiful Thing* as the sixth case study, as you will see, next.

CASE STUDY 6: THE COMING OUT STORY

BEAUTIFUL THING (1996)

Written by: Jonathan Harvey
Directed by: Hettie Macdonald
Produced by: Tony Garnett
Budget: £1.5 million

Q: What's good about it?

A: A gentle tale about love, which teens and adults alike can relate to, but which does not indulge in the sensational or the overly sentimental.

MY LOGLINE: When a young teenage boy's abused school friend comes to stay, the two lads realise new feelings and why they both never quite 'fitted in' with their peers.

Writing and Selling *Beautiful Thing*

In the late nineties, the UK was known for romantic comedy and hard-hitting drama. It was a very far cry from the current climate! In this age of austerity, genre can be highly prized, with low-budget horror, thriller and comedy on many agents', producers' and execs' wish lists. Yet when listening to any writer or producing team talk about their produced drama, it soon becomes apparent that getting the green light for drama has always been difficult. There's nearly always a fear the subject matter is too controversial, or conversely too dull; or that themes are not universal enough; or that audiences will not relate to the content, the characters or their world views. In short, drama is just a hard sell!

So, as I've said already, it's not so much a case of waiting for the 'right time', but MAKING that right time yourself: you have to ensure others share your vision and get on board WITH you. One way of 'making' that right time for your drama screenplay is by adapting it from another source. In the case of 1996's *Beautiful Thing*, it was originally written (and performed) as a stage play. The play is a classic coming of age tale, but unusually (especially for 1996) it does not focus on heterosexual love, but a burgeoning romance between two young, working-class teenagers, the bookish Jamie and 'lad's lad' Ste: 'I'd never written a screenplay before, so at first I was crap at it,' writer Jonathan Harvey confesses. 'It ended up being like a really shit, really long episode of *Grange Hill*!' The stage play is set entirely on the estate where its two would-be young lovers live, taking place inside a bedroom and the walkway outside. In comparison, the film takes in a number of locations, including both the boys' flats (as well as their neighbour Leah's); the bar where Jamie's mum, Sandra, works; Jamie and Ste's school; various walkways, the street and even the flats' terraces. Even so, *Beautiful Thing* still has its roots very firmly in its source material, thanks to director Hettie Macdonald: 'When Hettie was brought on to direct, she encouraged me to make it more like the play and only expand it when I needed to... keeping the claustrophobia of the play helped the screenplay become more focused,' Jonathan explains. This notion of keeping your own drama 'focused' is crucial, especially when it comes to keeping the budget down. Imaginative use of limited characters and locations can showcase your writing ability, especially if you can do this without compromising your story. In comparison, too many of the spec drama screenplays I read feel like potential 'stages on screen', with characters walking on simply to speak their lines, before exiting again.

By today's standards, £1.5 million is a huge whack of money for a realist drama. I'd wager it's unlikely an 'ardently British' drama feature like *Beautiful Thing* would receive the same amount of funding today: Film Four seems to prefer to fund more 'global' (adapted) dramas like *Slumdog Millionaire* and *12 Years a Slave*. It's also worth contrasting the budget of *Night People* from this book, which received far less public money. *Beautiful Thing* and *Night People* share another element as well: they both cast 'unknowns'. As with any film, casting is a huge issue for dramas, though for the opposite reason to many other genres, like thriller and comedy, which often thrive on spending money on so-called 'star power'. Making a realist drama like *Beautiful Thing* is markedly different in that it will frequently make use of those actors without 'names', not only for obvious financial reasons, but also in a bid to ensure audiences don't get 'taken out' of the story. Though Jonathan heard lots of suggestions for stars to play the mum, Sandra, in *Beautiful Thing*, its producer Tony Garnett said to Jonathan: 'People need to go to the pictures and see it and believe every second. The minute they think, "Oh look, there's so-and-so, pretending she lives in a council house", you've lost them.' Eventually the role went to Linda Henry, famous now for playing Shirley Carter in *EastEnders*.

It should also be noted the making of *Beautiful Thing* is a tale of perseverance. After it was initially rejected by Film Four, the play's rave reviews changed everything: 'Film Four called me back in and said they wanted to make it into a film... they gave me carte blanche to go round interviewing producers and production companies and deciding who I wanted to produce it,' Jonathan says. 'I realise now this was very unusual but I had no idea at the time!' Shot in a real housing estate, there were many issues in getting the film physically produced, in the middle of summer. Having worked there already, Jonathan knew the location and the people well, which helped. Jonathan tells me the night shoots were gruelling and it was hard to keep residents happy at two in the morning; location-wise, one of the flats used in the film is also Thamesmead Rape Crisis Centre, which was apparently 'shut for August'. The references to existing copyrighted material like *Coronation Street* (amusingly, Jonathan now works on *Corrie*) and the songs, such as the Mama Cass records Leah plays, or those which form part of the non-diegetic soundtrack, would have been expensive: some songs can cost thousands in rights! But without Mama Cass, Leah would have been a shadow of her former self from the source material. What's more, that famous dance scene at the end of the movie proved the biggest challenge: 'It was nerve wracking for everyone as there were only a handful of extras and the rest were real people who turned up to watch,' Jonathan says. 'You've got two teenage lads slow dancing to Mama Cass full blast and a crowd watching. In 1995! But they all got into the spirit of it, really.'

My Take on *Beautiful Thing*

Being the 'outsider' is a common feeling for teenagers, so even though *Beautiful Thing* is the best part of 20 years old now (thus practically 'coming of age' itself!), the core question at the heart of the story – 'Why do I not fit in?' – is still very relevant. We join the movie with Jamie attempting to play football, but being rejected by the other boys who throw homophobic insults his way. Jamie decides to mug off the day and slopes home to the London estate he shares with the other colourful characters who will be the main players in *Beautiful Thing*, such as neighbour Ste (whom we saw on the football field with the other boys who abused Jamie) and school dropout Leah, who now spends all her time playing Mama Cass records and complaining she's bored. What's perhaps most striking for me about *Beautiful Thing* is that the 'coming out' arc is not the protagonist's. We already know Jamie is gay from the first scene in the movie, and though he's not really sure yet how he feels or what to do about it, crucially Jamie knows he is gay too. Instead, it is love interest Ste, a secondary character, who must recognise himself as gay. In contrast, though the budding relationship between Ste and Jamie is the 'catalyst' for what transpires in *Beautiful Thing*, I would venture our protagonist's journey really lies in the resolution of the existing conflict between him and Sandra, his mother.

Jamie is the quiet, thoughtful only child of the brassy, larger-than-life Sandra who works in a bar and wants more out of life, not only for herself, but for Jamie too. The spec drama screenplays I read frequently focus on mother/child relationships (especially those with sons), often ignoring fathers altogether (who will often be absent from the narrative instead). Those mothers in the spec drama screenplays will often fall into two loose categories:

- *Neglectful Mother.* She likes booze, sex, drugs, WHATEVER a lot better than her kid. She doesn't cook, wash clothes or do anything mothers are 'supposed' to do; she swears, she smokes and is usually ill-educated. If she works, she works in a bar or club, sometimes as a barmaid, though also a pole dancer or stripper. Sometimes she's a criminal, handling stolen goods and the like. Occasionally she is well educated and then she's a workaholic, preferring her work as (usually) an accountant or similar to her child. She smokes a lot and may sweep into rooms to have a go at our young protagonist, who dreams of escaping her cruel grip.

- *Depressed Mother.* Depressed mother has too many children and can't handle it. We know this because she will spend a lot of time in bed, or staring out of windows; there will be moments in the screenplay when she screams at everyone about how she can't cope, and perhaps she delivers long monologues about how different (read: better) her life was before having children. Our protagonist is the eldest and has to look after his or her siblings, taking them to school and picking them up, even cooking their tea and ensuring they get in the bath.

Combined with that very two-dimensional characterisation, the spec drama screenplay mother above will usually have a very peripheral role in the narrative. A favourite storyline is our protagonist stealing money or a car and then running away from their mother, for whatever reason. Occasionally there is a big confrontation between them, where our hero/ine pleads with his/her mother to really see what is going on with their lives that may or may not relate to the story situation they find themselves in. In short, both versions of the spec drama mother character (and even fathers, by their absence) are put under the spotlight and found wanting. I'm sure scribes don't mean it this way, but the lack of variety here means quite a damning statement is made.

At first glance, Sandra appears to be the 'classic' working-class mother who appears in this type of drama: she smokes, she drinks, she swears; she even works in a bar. But unlike the many spec drama screenplays I read, Sandra occupies a huge part of the story and plays a pivotal role in both Jamie and Ste's emotional growth in the course of the narrative of *Beautiful Thing*, in the following ways:

- **She's funny.** Sandra is not a comic relief character, but she is funny. She mocks Jamie, Leah and even her own boyfriend, the hippy clod Lenny. One of my favourite moments is when she takes the phone to talk to one of Jamie's teachers, yet again: 'Hello. I believe you wanted to talk to me about my total git of a son?' As the mother of a teenage boy myself, I have uttered these words, too – if not aloud, then definitely in my head.

- **She's sharp.** Very often, mums in the spec drama screenplays I read are cast adrift by circumstance; they're poor and have no way out. In comparison, Sandra may not a well-educated woman, but she is ambitious and clever. When she is offered the job at the pub, we can see why; she's canny enough to get in advance the 'insider info' necessary to impress the board of bosses. Jamie has a slight superiority complex when it comes to Sandra; he thinks he's cleverer than her, like most teenagers. There's a strong moment when Sandra warns him, a dangerous smile on her face, 'Don't make out I'm thick, Jamie.' We wouldn't dare!

- **She's emotional.** The first word we hear from Sandra's lips is 'Slag!', levied at Leah. Why a grown woman would have a vendetta with a school leaver is up for interpretation. Leah is cited AND shown as being a nuisance predominantly for playing her records at such loud volumes, not to mention she is also a shit stirrer, which is illustrated later when Leah tells Lenny (incorrectly) that Sandra aborted his baby. Incensed and hurt, Sandra does not wait to confront Leah; instead she marches round to the party Jamie and all his friends are at, to tell Leah it was actually a miscarriage (after assaulting her!). Jamie is mortified by his mother's behaviour, not considering Sandra's feelings as a human being, earning (rightfully) the sharp side of her tongue as well. This is a recurring conflict between them throughout the movie, in which she defends herself, on one occasion even raining frustrated (albeit light) blows on him. In other words, Sandra does her best and Jamie says it's not good enough. This is a brilliant touch, because this is something (good) parents and their teenagers face every day: it's authentic and feels real. So we empathise with Sandra, not Jamie, because Jamie is unduly harsh on his mother, as teenagers are typically wont to be. Yet the spec drama screenplays I read nearly always place a line in the sand between the teenager and the parent the reverse way: the parent is not interested in his/her child, they want it done 'their way or the high way', so we want the teen to get away.

- **Sandra is still on Jamie's side.** Sandra is on Jamie's case throughout the movie, whether it's his truancy, doing his homework, wondering where he's been or how he's going to cope as a gay man in a hostile world. But, again, these are all things GOOD parents worry about, even if teenagers don't see what the big deal is, or think that it's none of their parents' business. Despite this, however, Sandra will do whatever it takes for her son, which includes lying to his teachers on the phone... though she will also teach him a lesson for putting her in that position!

- **Sandra is a Good Samaritan.** Walking home from work one night, she discovers a morose Ste sitting by himself by the water: he's received yet another beating from his father, Ronnie, this time for burning the dinner. Taking Ste home with her, Sandra announces Ste will be 'top and tailing it' with Jamie, before shouting through the letterbox next door to the unimpressed and abusive Ronnie that she's looking after his son. So, in other words, Sandra is the catalyst for the story: had she not got involved, Ste and Jamie would never have been thrown together so intimately. This is interesting, because in most of the drama specs I read, if mother characters are there at all, they're usually simply orbiting around the teenagers, not kicking off the story.

- **The conflict is not what we expect.** It would be very easy to have caused conflict between Sandra and Jamie by having her oblivious, or disapproving of him and/or his 'way of life'. But Sandra knows her son is 'not like other boys' and there's a poignant moment in the flat's living room when Jamie challenges her to say he's 'weird': 'No... you're alright. YOU'RE ALRIGHT,' she insists. We sense that Sandra accepts who Jamie is absolutely and this is illustrated perfectly in the resolution of the movie when she dances with Leah, as Jamie and Ste slow dance in front of all the other tenement residents. Instead, the conflict comes from Sandra's concerns for Jamie, as an out gay man in a world that will not always be as accepting as she is.

On the surface, *Beautiful Thing* could have been your average nineties depressing drama: we've got poor teenagers; a housing estate; single mum; domestic abuse; smoking, swearing and drinking! Yet *Beautiful Thing* handles all this, plus its gay love story, with a whimsical, almost tongue-in-cheek vibe throughout. Again, it would have been so easy for Jamie and Ste to embark on a doomed love affair, further underlining that being a homosexual in today's Britain is an isolating and painful experience. Yet *Beautiful Thing* sidesteps this predictable storyline with ease, instead showing us that acceptance, tolerance and understanding are indeed beautiful things.

What We Can Learn from *Beautiful Thing*

Write Tips:

- On the surface, *Beautiful Thing* may look like a 'typical' British film set in an urban area, but nothing can be further from the truth. Sometimes we can subvert expectations by seemingly giving producers, filmmakers and audiences what they purport to want, but with our own motivations firmly in mind. So if you feel that a certain group of people is underserved by drama, or are sick of stereotypes or particular 'kinds' of stories, go for it. In 1996, there had not been many stories about gay romances, which contributed to the success of *Beautiful Thing*. Can you think of a real-life issue or topic that has not been covered much (or only in one way) and bring it to life? If you can, you may find your drama story has people queueing up to help you!

- In order to do the above, make sure your characters are not 'the usual', but don't make them so far out of left field that they're totally unrecognisable either. Sandra works so well because she is what we expect, but in a totally new way. Her boyfriend, Lenny, isn't the 'usual' addict boyfriend and domestic abuser we might expect, either; nor is Jamie the average drama protagonist, agonising over his homosexuality.

- *Beautiful Thing* is arguably as whimsical as *Juno*, yet this is a tone and story world script readers and filmmakers see very infrequently in British drama screenplays in the spec pile. Light and shade is SO important to drama, yet that misunderstanding amongst writers over 'depressing drama' continues to dominate spec screenplays. Whilst there's nothing wrong with a good old-fashioned DEVASTATING drama, I'd venture a screenwriter is better off writing optimistic stories in order to get noticed, which means a stack more research is needed by writers in terms of watching them!

Selling Points:

- If you want to subvert expectation, you're probably not the only one frustrated with the current status quo. Remember Gail Hackston's 'unusual' cancer story, or the fact Noel Clarke was angry enough to write a screenplay 'setting the record straight' about how young people 'really' are... if you feel strongly about something, chances are others do too. So think of a story you're passionate about and find others who are just as passionate. This is a shared dream, not just yours.

- It's unlikely a realist British drama would be awarded as much as £1.5 million nowadays, so think of ways you can achieve something similar to *Beautiful Thing* for much less (i.e. £50,000–£500,000, like *Night People* and *Kidulthood*). Casting can be an issue for dramas, but in the opposite way to genre films: you may actively want unknown actors.

- Limited characters and locations are generally a must for a micro-budget to low-budget drama screenplay: 5–6 characters maximum and 3–4 locations is optimum. However, if you can make a few locations seem like more, or use a large cast in interesting ways (such as asking schools, youth groups or estate residents to 'turn up' and agree to being filmed, perhaps in return for food or drink), there are always ways round this if your producer is willing to think creatively. And do remember that, if you're shooting on location, it helps if you know the area and its people well as you can use the goodwill you've generated.

- The songs in *Beautiful Thing* would have been very costly, just as all the snippets and references to *Mary Poppins* would have been in *Saving Mr Banks*. If you 'need' to include music in a realist drama spec feature screenplay, can you think of an alternative, e.g. a character is a singer-songwriter, who writes his/her own material? If that will not work, make sure you have a rock-solid story reason why your drama screenplay cannot do without it.

- Adaptations of plays can offer very real opportunities for spec drama screenplays: if your play does well, people are more likely to want you to make the film version. Look into staging your own and/or working with small theatre companies, many of which encourage new writers.

TRUE BLUE

WHAT IS 'CHARACTER CHANGE'?

'Character change' is something lauded a lot online as a 'good' thing (especially by so-called writing 'gurus' and courses), regardless of the story being told. To be honest, I'm ambivalent about character change when it comes to genre screenplays; I even argue some of the most iconic protagonists, especially in thrillers and horrors of the last 30 years, hardly change at all. So, as with all writing endeavours, I don't think a 'one size fits all' approach is either useful or necessary. And in the case of spec genre screenplays, this addiction to supposed 'character change' has actually created a load of NEW problems for those writers, because I have noticed a very sudden upturn in the spec pile of completely unnecessary prologues! In a bid to satisfy the gurus, box-ticking scribes desperately try to 'shoe-horn in' supposedly 'character-building' pasts (especially tragic ones), so their protagonists might 'change', regardless of whether the story warrants it or not. And guess what happens? Do we think, 'Oh, I've seen WHY this character is a headcase; now I automatically care about him/her'? No, we do not. We are instead impatient, waiting for the story to start. This is NEVER a good idea when it comes to a spec genre screenplay, where it's demanded we 'hit the ground running'. In comparison, dramas frequently have protagonists who 'change' in some way, though often not in the way spec screenwriters might assume. Relying on that notion of a character's (tragic) past will frequently do as little for the drama screenplay protagonist as it does for the one in the genre script, because prologues in any screenplay frequently perform a plot or story function, rather than a character one. What's more, dramas need to 'hit the ground running' every bit as much as genre screenplays, because the demand is the same: do not bore us by making us wait!

DEVASTATING IS NOT A SYNONYM

Because of so many writers' and filmmakers' misunderstanding of what 'struggle' entails in drama, I want to break down precisely why *Blue Valentine* is 'devastating' and NOT depressing. On this basis, I will walk through what ALL spec drama screenplays should do to get the reader or audience on board, using *Blue Valentine* as an example with reference, not only to its concept and characters, but also to its logline, structure and the message (or 'point') behind the story.

First, ALL spec drama screenplays should do the following three things:

- *Introduce us to the characters and story TOGETHER.* The story of a marriage breakdown, we join the story of *Blue Valentine* with the couple's little girl, Frankie. She crawls through the dog door – why isn't the door opened for her?? – and wakes her father Dean (Gosling), who is asleep on the sofa. He is a devoted dad and immediately helps her look for the family dog, which is apparently lost. He goes outside, holding her, and beyond the house we see an open space of grass, which Frankie then runs out into. It is to all intents and purposes a beautiful scene: the sun is shining bright, the little girl is gorgeous, dressed in her finery, and we think, 'The dog will turn up... any second... now.' But it doesn't. This seems a little odd, but we accept the dog not showing up, and Frankie runs back across the field, looking very much like she belongs in a John Singer Sargent painting. Dean plays with Frankie; they pretend to be tigers. They go through to the bedroom where the mother, Cindy (Michelle Williams), is asleep. In comparison to Dean, Cindy is not happy to be woken, yet Dean and Frankie don't appear to notice this. We expect Cindy to remember herself and go, 'Oh, you guys!' and join in, but she doesn't. Instead she insists, 'I'm SLEEPING!', pulling the duvet over her head. This immediately gets us thinking again: where is the dog? Why is Frankie looking for it on her own, whilst her parents sleep? Why are the parents not asleep TOGETHER, whether on the sofa or in the bedroom? This sequence is only two or three minutes maximum on screen and occupies little space on the actual page, yet says EVERYTHING about the characters and where they are in the world at this moment, as we join the story.

- **Start as it means to go on.** Consider your own favourite dramas. Where do they begin? What is the first image we see? Most screenplays have no real 'opener' that sets the tone for the film. Instead, characters will be sitting thinking about 'stuff' or being miserable in some way. Now contrast this again with *Blue Valentine*'s opening image: a beautiful little girl, worried about a lost dog. It's the story of a marriage breakdown, thus suddenly such a scene feels ominous, as we also figure even more will be lost as the story continues, which of course it is. What's more, as the movie continues, we discover the dog does not return because it is dead: Cindy finds the deceased animal on the way to Frankie's school play. When she arrives, crying, Dean does not wait for Cindy's explanation but chastises her for being late. The dog is essentially Cindy and Dean's marriage: it's dead, but they just don't realise it yet.

- **Where does it end?** Despite its complex, non-linear storytelling, *Blue Valentine* is 'bookended' – it ends as it begins, with Frankie, shouting after her father Dean as he walks away. This is a masterstroke of good storytelling because it underlines that whatever Cindy might receive in terms of personal space and peace of mind by breaking up with Dean at last, her gain is Frankie's loss. Children are so often overlooked in stories about divorce (especially via the assumption, 'It's better for them this way, not so many arguments'), so *Blue Valentine* not only makes a refreshing change by including Frankie's POV, it also adds to our devastation that Cindy and Dean could not make it work, despite both their best efforts. Frankie is the ultimate 'lost girl'.

WHAT IS A TRANSFORMATIVE ARC?

Spec screenwriters (and many produced ones, incidentally) appear set on 'character change' in recent years as a solely 'positive' thing. With the deluge of 'tragic pasts' it would seem writers want their characters to 'vanquish' their fears and/or deal with their past losses. That is obviously no bad thing (especially when it comes to challenging accepted norms and values through well-conceived characterisation and plotting), but again it's about differentiation against the rest of the spec pile. Often, the most memorable drama screenplays are those with characters who experience that inevitable descent into the negative, as mentioned in the section on the theme of 'devastation'. This is especially the case in indie film. In typical Hollywoodised fare, for example, Dean and Cindy in *Blue Valentine* would resolve their issues, rather than split up. Instead, we see the problem is thus: Cindy DOES change, but Dean stays exactly where he is. Arguably, Cindy is bitter and put-upon; perhaps if she had chilled out as Dean suggests, their marriage might have been saved. After everything that has happened in their lives together, however, she doesn't feel she can stay still, and that's not her fault. Equally, Dean isn't at fault either: this is just who he is and Cindy knew that when she married him. Dean's personality and world view worked for Cindy back when she was a student and needed him to 'legitimise' Frankie by taking her on as his own child. The issue behind the story we're watching, then, is that Dean's laissez-faire attitude no longer works for Cindy in the present day, and even though Dean does not want to split up, he cannot provide his wife with what she needs: they have reached an impasse and there is quite literally no way back. *Blue Valentine* is the story of Cindy making that realisation and forcing the issue that leads to that impasse. Though we join Cindy in bed and annoyed – 'I'm sleeping!' – she's not at that stage yet where she realises Dean is no longer right for her. There's still a small part of her that hopes this is just a rough patch and they can work their way out of it, hence her agreeing to go away with him for the night (the 'Blue Valentine' of the title is the ridiculous 'robot's vagina' in a hotel's science-fiction-themed suite).

Over the course of the narrative Cindy DOES change... not for the 'better', but arguably not for the worse, either. In the long term, her decision to split with Dean may indeed work out best for everyone (though it's important to note that this idea goes beyond the storyline of the movie we are watching). All the negative elements of Cindy and Dean's personalities clash in the impressive scene in the sonographer's office. Convinced he can change Cindy's mind, Dean storms in and insists on reconciliation. Yet if there was ever a chance of saving their marriage, it's at this precise moment everything goes downhill and all is lost. Her career is the only thing Cindy has that is 'Dean free'; for him to invade it makes her mind up once and for all, leading her to yell at him, 'I hate you!... you cunt!' On this basis, then, when it comes to great drama storytelling, the concept of 'character change' should arguably come without a built-in judgement. This is why I do not talk of 'character change' (especially since writers seem so set on this being 'a good thing'), but 'transformative arcs':

Characters start in one place... but end up in another.

This movement may happen purposefully or accidentally (to the character in question, at least). In addition, beyond society's accepted norms and values ('Thou Shalt Not Kill' being the most obvious), the judgement on a character's actions and world view should be the audience's, NOT the writer's or filmmaker's. For example, I believe absolutely that neither Cindy nor Dean is at fault in *Blue Valentine* and they both act as heinously as each other.

However, I have argued many times with friends who believe Dean is a waster and should 'man up'; or that Cindy is a martyr and a bad mother for kicking Frankie's father out. *Blue Valentine* is a layered enough drama to support ALL THREE of these interpretations – and probably more, too. Yet spec drama screenplays often fail to grab readers because there is just one way of viewing a situation: someone is at fault, another person is not, and the answer to a dilemma (or similar) is 'obvious'. If you want to elicit an authentic emotional response from your reader (and thus your audience), nothing should EVER be 'obvious'. Make your characters 'transform', make them face unpalatable things about themselves and others via that notion of 'internal conflict', which in turn will ensure the actions of the story point to the psyches of those characters, a perfect circle. But how to go about tackling a 'transformative arc'? Try asking yourself these questions:

- *What is my character like at the beginning of the story, and at the end?* Writers frequently draw characters in very broad strokes when it comes to this element of their drama screenplays. A character who is repugnant at the beginning will usually reform by the end; or a timid mouse of a person will become brave and courageous. But the best drama screenplays explore the psyche of these characters and draw attention to those minute changes within the person that mean the world to them, but aren't necessarily obvious immediately to the outside world... the audience shares in the character's journey, then, every step of the way.

- *Why do I want him/her to make this realisation/change/choice (or not, as the case may be)?* In comparison to genre film, in which a protagonist does not necessarily have to change over the course of a narrative, a drama character usually must confront something metaphorical about themselves, the world or people around them. Remember, though we begin with an obvious problem between Cindy and Dean, via their flashbacks we discover that they started off very much in love: Dean is

Cindy's hero – at first. He's a veritable knight in shining armour, taking on someone else's child as his own and validating her as a woman for the first time. Fast-forward a few years and it's a very different story: Dean has let himself go, complacent; Cindy feels trapped and resentful. Despite both of their best efforts, their relationship is doomed and, crucially, both make an attempt to resurrect the relationship, as well as behaving badly. This is not only realistic; it allows people in the audience to relate to this story by comparing it to their own relationship breakdowns, meaning that the all-important emotional response can occur, a triple whammy of great drama writing. I don't mind admitting I cried like a baby at the end of *Blue Valentine*, as Dean strides off down the street, daughter Frankie calling after him, the only dad she has ever known, as fireworks go off where people elsewhere in the city celebrate.

- *What am I trying to say here?* Any writing of any kind is in essence a communication and it's more than possible to create insightful messages and themes in genre stories. However, it is not essential, especially when we consider the primary function of genre film is entertainment. If the primary function of drama film is that all-important emotional response in the audience, we need to keep in mind how we are going to induce that, right from the outset. In other words, we need to know WHY we want to tell the story we have chosen; WHAT the story means to us; WHO it will appeal to; and WHY we feel it is important to share this 'message'.

DRAMA LOGLINES

Loglines are always difficult to write, but especially so for drama screenplays because too often they seem too 'small' at best and horribly depressing at worst, meaning they're an extremely hard sell in terms of grabbing someone's attention. Considering *Blue Valentine* again, check out this one, which I found on a film review site:

The film depicts a married couple, Dean and Cindy, shifting back and forth in time between their courtship and the dissolution of their marriage several years later. (27 words)

If I heard this pitch at the London Screenwriters' Festival, or received it via email, I would probably NOT request the screenplay. It's not the worst logline I've ever read, but it does very little to sell the film 'off the page' to me... and yet I love *Blue Valentine*! So let's rewrite it.

Perhaps the most intriguing thing about *Blue Valentine* is the fact it's non-linear: the marriage breakdown is set in 'the present' and contrasted with the hopeful burgeoning of romance back in 'the past'. Yet, crucially, the beginnings of Dean and Cindy's love is not all 'moonlight and roses': Cindy is pregnant by a musclehead jock at her university and almost goes through with an abortion she doesn't want; similarly, the jock beats on Dean for daring to 'steal' his woman. What's more, both Cindy and Dean are flawed, troubled individuals with lots of emotional baggage of their own, plus they're from two very different backgrounds. We know relatively little about Dean, other than that he is (we assume) a badly educated, blue-collar worker, with relatively few aspirations. In comparison, Cindy is a high achiever, desperate for something 'more' in her life. Having yearned to be a doctor, she ends up making do instead with being a sonographer, her ambitions cut short by marrying Dean so young (rather than having daughter Frankie, a clever reversal of expectation here). It's Dean, not the baby, who becomes a millstone around Cindy's neck: there's a brilliant scene in which Cindy says Dean has 'so much potential', but she's describing herself and her own clipped wings more than she is him and his job painting houses. Dean takes her and his family for granted: he 'rescued' Cindy from the jock and from her own belief she was not lovable – it doesn't get any better, right? And for Cindy it quite literally doesn't... which is why she grows to hate Dean, a real modern tragedy that so many in the audience can relate to. So, thinking about all of this, the words that pop out at me are: non-linear... love... married couple... hate... tragedy. So here's my rewritten logline:

A non-linear tragedy, in which a young couple's marriage breakdown is contrasted against the heady early days of their relationship, yet because of their very different outlooks and backgrounds, and despite both their good intentions, love soon turns to hate. (40 words)

I believe this is a much better pitch for *Blue Valentine* because it illustrates both its method of storytelling (non-linear) and the characters' arcs within it. Whilst some people might be of the view this story sounds 'depressing' due to the 'love turns to hate' aspect, it's important to remember hate is an active state of being, just as love is (hence there being a 'thin line' between them), plus *Blue Valentine* does not have a 'happy ever after', so to leave out 'love turns to hate' or the word 'tragedy' could be viewed as disingenuous. We are MEANT to be devastated by that ending, by Dean walking off into the distance, by Frankie's calls after him; the writer leads us to believe the situation might be salvaged right till the last possible second. My tears were what the writer and filmmaker wanted, but crucially I wasn't depressed by that ending: I found it cathartic. I was remembering the various break-ups and near break-ups I've had, but also thinking of how, although it might have seemed like the end of the world at the time, everything had turned out okay in the end. And that is the true power of a good drama screenplay. In crafting your OWN drama screenplay logline, consider the following:

- **What type of drama is this?** If drama is 'everything else' that doesn't come under the banner of high-concept, event-driven genre film, you need to give a nod to what type of drama story you're telling. In the case of *Blue Valentine*, I needed to mention it is non-linear and deals with contrast (i.e. good to bad times), but if yours is a true story, mockumentary or whimsical dramedy, why not give an indication of this in your logline?

- **Who are my characters?** Remember, your characters are undergoing something deeply personal and your conflict is likely to be internal, rather than external. But DON'T fall back on cliché, whatever you do! Look at my logline for *Blue Valentine* again: I describe their issues as being differing 'outlooks and backgrounds', but crucially I also draw attention to the fact that we are supposed to sympathise with them BOTH, not one over the other, with 'despite both their good intentions'. If you're used to writing loglines for genre films, you'll likely know 'the shorter the better' is the ideal, something in the region of twenty-five words. Drama loglines are typically longer, since they need to be 'character-led', like the stories they represent. The ideal in my opinion is 35 to 40 words, though there are always exceptions: true stories lend themselves pretty well to shorter loglines, I find.

- *What emotional response do I want from my audience and how will I go about it?* *Blue Valentine* is a tragedy; we're supposed to be devastated by its conclusion and wish it could be different for Dean and Cindy. But including 'the heady early days of their relationship' hints that *Blue Valentine* will not be a feature-length misery fest, as does 'their good intentions': there are moments of humour and warmth to the movie, such as when Dean quizzes Cindy when he first meets her, or when she dances to his ukulele and terrible singing in the doorway. Most importantly, it's these moments that make us wish it could have worked out for them. Love it or hate it, *Blue Valentine* is a masterclass in devastating drama BECAUSE of light and shade, not in spite of it.

NO ONE SIZE FITS ALL

CHANGE AGENTS

As with all elements of creative writing, there are always exceptions and, in the case of drama screenplays and transformative arcs, it is important to note there are drama protagonists whose function is to stay exactly the same. These 'change agents' instead inspire other characters to make realisations about their lives and the world around them. The most obvious 'change agent' is, of course, the title character of *Forrest Gump* (1994), whose unyieldingly optimistic (and simplistic) view of life transforms the lives of secondary characters such as Bubba, Lieutenant Dan and Jenny, not to mention countless peripheral characters, either forever or momentarily. Forrest is present at a number of historic moments and is directly responsible for a number of iconic pop culture elements, from Elvis's trademark jig to 'Shit Happens' car bumper stickers, underlining the message of the film that we ALL have the capacity to make an impact on others' lives. Though *Forrest Gump* is frequently talked down as being 'overly sentimental' and even 'sick making', it was the winner of six Academy Awards, including Best Picture and, most importantly, remains a hugely popular movie with audiences some 20 years later. In a world that may seem cold and intimidating to so many, a 'feel-good' movie that draws attention to the fact we DON'T have to 'transform' ourselves in order to matter to other people is obviously hugely important to audiences. As writers, then, we must not underestimate change agents in our bid for great characterisation for our spec drama screenplays.

'CLOSED' PROTAGONISTS

Another method of characterisation, other than transformative arcs and change agents, worth thinking about is the notion of what I call the 'closed protagonist'. Sometimes these protagonists are called 'passive', which is a term I ultimately disagree with, because usually they will have to make some kind of decision at some point in the narrative for a specific reason, even if it is only once (thus meaning they do contribute actively to the story). What is notable then about the closed protagonist in drama screenplays is not that they're literally 'closed off' (though sometimes they are, as in the case of the title character in *Dumbo* [1941] who is completely silent), but the fact that another character – usually a secondary, though sometimes an antagonist – will need to 'take the reins' of the story FOR them for an extended period, often half or even two thirds of the story. In Dumbo's case, his mouse friend, Timothy, communicates to us, the audience, the elephant's desperate need and desire, not only to be back with his mother, but to be liked and accepted for who he is, big ears and all (and both of these dreams come true by the end of the film).

In the case of *Sideways* (2004), however, it is antagonist, Jack, not closed protagonist, Miles, who drives the drama... It is Jack's bachelor party Miles is present at, not his own; plus it is the fallout Jack creates that Miles must deal with, especially when it comes to hiding Jack's infidelity from his fiancée so her feelings are spared. Throughout the entire movie Miles puts aside his own needs in favour of others', creating obstacle after obstacle for himself, so he is unable to engage with his own desire to be loved. It is only in the last few moments of the film that Miles finally decides to take a chance with Maya. We finish the story with him on her doorstep; we don't even know how it will turn out (especially given his brittle and infuriating behaviour with Maya earlier). Ultimately, the emotional response elicited by both *Dumbo* and *Sideways*, made over 60 years apart, one animated, the other live action, is again one of hope for the future.

STRUCTURE

Many screenwriters erroneously believe characterisation to be the most important element of the character-led drama screenplay. But whether a character has a transformative arc, or is a change agent or closed protagonist, *structure* must play its part in bringing his or her story to us, the audience. Yet a huge proportion of spec drama screenplays have their characters essentially 'stand still': they quite literally want or desire nothing. As a result their stories feel like extended sessions of 'talking heads' and I feel as if I'm reading screenplays filled with various people talking about 'stuff'. Some of it is even interesting, but only in the sense some drunk person chatting randomly to you on the bus can be entertaining on occasion... it's very hit or miss – and usually a big fat MISS.

So, how best to tackle structure, when it comes to your own spec drama screenplay? Frustratingly, there are no genre conventions to draw from; just like its story, theme and characters, a drama screenplay can use whatever it wants in terms of structural methods (as long as that is what's best for the story). Knowing where to start, then, can be difficult and brain exploding, because arguably you *could* tell it any number of ways! Again, it's a question of listening to your gut and remembering what excited you about the story when you first conceived it. You must also identify those threats and opportunities that will not only get your screenplay written, but help sell it 'off the page' to others, including the audience.

In the course of my research for this book and watching a stack of produced dramas, I would venture movies may fall into one of the following three (very) loose structural categories:

- *Linear.* As its name suggests, linear storytelling is the 'typical' or 'usual' way of telling a story, with a beginning, middle and end in the 'right' order. How a spec screenwriter tackles structure in their drama screenplay will ultimately be up to them (I'm a 'three acts' girl myself, as everyone knows); but perhaps more surprisingly, *how* that linear tale will be interpreted structurally will be up to the person reading and/or viewing it. Many spec drama screenwriters will write to me, telling me to look at their screenplays with reference to a particular structural method, but the fact is, I don't really 'get' how structure works beyond The Three Acts. That's not to say I don't understand alternative versions; of course I do. But when I look at anyone's linear story, I think 'Beginning, Middle, End' with a catalyst into the middle (or 'plot point', if you like), a midpoint (halfway, page-wise), and a further catalyst that spurs us on to the end (or 'plot point two'). That's it. Why complicate things? But that's just me. Fact is, you can call your structural method whatever you want and follow whatever diagrams/instructions make most sense to you! NEVER listen to the people who tell you you're doing it 'wrong' or that your draft is 'doomed' if you don't use whatever it is they're hocking. Page counting and getting hysterical over where events are 'supposed' to be is not the way forward. Have faith in your ability to tell a story. After all, the only things readers (and thus audiences) care about is that a story a) makes sense and b) is interesting!

- *Non-linear.* A good proportion of spec drama screenplays are non-linear. That is in itself unremarkable when we consider how drama stories are frequently about the psyche (with the likes of flashbacks placing us 'inside' characters' minds); or else they involve large swathes of time, which means they may utilise a device like the framing story. Many spec screenwriters get confused about flashbacks and framing stories, but they are not the same. Flashbacks are usually short sequences, sometimes momentary intercuts, taking us back in time for some reason relating to plot and/or character (especially if their POV changes). In comparison, a framing story relates most often to plot structure. The most classic version in a drama screenplay and/or produced content is a character who is now old in the so-called 'present', telling his or her story to a younger character... and then we move into the 'past', to see that older character as a young man or woman, or perhaps another character altogether! Typically we will rejoin that older character not only at the end, but at various points throughout the narrative, especially for comedic or dramatic purposes. Framing stories were particularly popular in eighties family dramas relating to characters reading books or fairy tales, such as Grandfather telling the story of *The Princess Bride* (1987) to his grandson, who is home from school, ill in bed. Last of all, and not to be underestimated, is the much-maligned dream sequence: we don't see it much outside of horror and the occasional thriller and I always wonder why, when its potential for drama is huge (when used well!).

- *Episodic.* If dealing with an epic arena or 'larger-than-life' character (or both), especially in the biopic of a famous person (but not necessarily), a spec drama screenwriter may elect to use an episodic structure. Usually those loosely connected 'episodes' of a person's life will relate back to the story's theme or overarching message in some way. In the case of *Forrest Gump*, the various episodes of his childhood involving his low IQ and his mother's unrelenting loyalty obviously 'feed into' what comes next. We believe he will not leave Lieutenant Dan or Bubba, becoming a war hero not because of patriotism or duty, but because of that same loyalty 'no matter what' Forrest's mother showed him as a child. Similarly, Forrest's later success on the football field cleverly mirrors his lack of success with Jenny as his love interest, because they are from two different worlds, both intellectually and emotionally. This is neatly tied in with Jenny's, 'Run, Forrest!,' in that renowned scene in which the child version of himself sheds his leg calipers running from the bullies. It should be noted here too that a spec TV drama pilot will most likely need to be episodic, especially if it is for a returning series, to accommodate its 'story of the week' and 'serial element'. That said, if a writer wants to attempt a feature-length drama screenplay for television, aka a 'movie of the week', the usual thoughts on structure apply with regard to non-linearity. Though MOWs don't tend to be made in the UK (and especially not from material by new writers), I have heard of spec screenwriters getting deals on their MOWs to develop them with prodcos and networks as returning series (though I've not knowingly seen any of the finished results on the small screen). In addition, MOW scripts can sell overseas, especially in the US and Germany, though a writer usually needs an agent to access these markets.

THE POINT OF NO RETURN

Various structural 'gurus' and methods talk of the concept of 'All Is Lost,' most famously Blake Snyder's 'Save the Cat!' structural breakdown. However, just like the notion of 'character change', this does not always necessarily reflect what a story needs in my opinion (especially drama screenplays in which writers want to elicit joy as an emotional response from their target audience). Instead, if we think about transformative arcs, or the choices change agents and closed protagonists may (or may not!) make, I think it's potentially more useful to think of 'The Point of No Return'. This is because produced drama content does not necessarily deal in 'life-or-death' stakes, because a drama's primary role is looking at characters' psyches and world views. So audiences are often asked to invest in a protagonist's more metaphorical goals, such as throwing off the shackles of the past, dealing with bereavement or loss, or 'winning' (whether that means actually winning at a contest or not). However, to be able to do this, there must be a moment where the plot 'tips' (a 'point of no return'), which then creates a shift in the dramatic context of the story and propels those characters towards the resolution. But what is dramatic context and how does it work in drama screenplays?

DRAMATIC CONTEXT

One of the most undervalued elements of the writing craft in general is dramatic context. If 'drama is conflict' the background or climate surrounding events in the story (the context) simply MUST change (regardless of whether characters do or not). If the characters in your spec drama screenplay are not to 'stand still', something must compel them to 'do something'. Again, obvious stuff, yet my experience is no different from that of various script readers the world over when I say the spec pile is filled to the brim with characters standing stock still!

THE THREE DRAMA SCREENPLAY STRUCTURES

But how do we find the 'dramatic context' of our stories, which will in turn help us pinpoint what kind of structure we use: linear, non-linear or episodic? Well, why not let your character do it for you?

- **Does your character have a 'transformative arc'?** They do? Great! Then this should be easiest for you, because, as we know, spec drama screenplays and produced content frequently include characters who make some sort of realisation over the course of the narrative. So, as an example, if your character goes from hopefulness to hopelessness (as Cindy does in *Blue Valentine*), then, quite simply, the dramatic context of your story reflects that. As a result, the first half or three quarters of your screenplay will reflect your character HOPING she can turn the situation around, with the second half or last quarter reflecting that, basically, EVERYTHING IS SCREWED.

  TIPS: Keep it simple. Don't lose sight of what's going on in your drama screenplay by trying to shove too much in there. Relate everything back to your dramatic context to ensure that your character, and what happens to him/her, stays on the straight and narrow. With all this in mind, then, characters with transformative arcs lend themselves particularly well to linear narratives... but this is where it gets complicated, because non-linear narratives also like characters with transformative arcs! Leading me to my next question...

- **Do you want to use a non-linear structure method?** Okay, so we've established your character has a transformative arc and you feel you want to use something non-linear in telling that character's story. Nothing wrong with that! Non-linearity typically gets a bad rap as a storytelling device amongst script readers, producers and filmmakers, often because a large proportion of spec screenplays do it BADLY. The function of non-linearity in any story, but especially a drama screenplay, is usually that the 'past' (or similar, whatever this means) must inform the 'present' (ditto) in some way with reference to the following:

i. What does the PAST tell us about the PRESENT in this story, in terms of a) plot, b) character, or c) both?

ii. What device are you using for the non-linearity? (i.e. flashback, framing story, dream sequence, etc., and HOW: it must be consistent!)

iii. Does the story NEED to be non-linear?

Working backwards (naturally!) and dealing with the third point first, I would venture the vast majority of non-linear screenplays do NOT need to be non-linear, and are that way simply because the writer has conceived of the storyline with 'style over substance' in mind. This is obviously not desirable, especially in drama where characterisation is so important. Moving on to the second point, then, it is important to ensure non-linearity follows its own structure, so the audience might have an 'anchor' on how it works: e.g. if all the flashbacks were cut out and edited together, would they form a complete short film of their own? Or are they the 'visual answers' to questions posed in the present? Or something else entirely? Finally, if we are to consider that non-linearity has its own function, i.e. that of pushing the 'present' story forward (rather than simply filling in gaps with extraneous exposition or character background), the first point must be adhered to, to the letter. The co-writer of *Saving Mr Banks*, Kelly Marcel, talks of 'rhythm' and 'feel', two things spec screenwriters attempting non-linearity frequently underestimate, preferring instead to rely on page counting and paradigms, or, conversely, random pot luck! But all this leads to a disjointed narrative, a big fat headache for your script reader, and development hell for your spec drama screenplay.

TIPS: If you want to attempt a non-linear narrative for your spec drama screenplay, write not one but TWO individual outlines or scene breakdowns: one listing the plot beats of the 'present' thread, the other the 'past' thread. You can then weave the two storylines together to the story's satisfaction (obviously, do this whatever way works for you, such as index cards, virtual or real, or a written list, which you can cut up and move around; or use a structure programme or tool online, and so on). From there, write a short outline of two to four pages incorporating all those plot beats (both 'present' and 'past', in the order you have decided). You're not writing a 'selling document', but an extended 'note to self' to see if the story works. Remember: if you cannot make it work on two to four pages, you cannot make it work on ninety to a hundred! Don't gloss over glitches and holes in the hope you can fix it in the actual screenplay later; all that will happen is you'll tie yourself and your story up in knots. Non-linearity IS hard, so don't sabotage yourself and your draft from the outset.

- *Is your character a change agent?* There's absolutely no reason a change agent cannot be part of a linear or non-linear storyline, but they arguably thrive better in episodic structures. The reason for this is simple. Thinking back again to *Forrest Gump*, we can believe in his status as a change agent because he affects SO MANY people's lives, whether they are close to him (Jenny, Lieutenant Dan, Bubba, his mother) or not (Elvis or the random joggers, 'Shit Happens'). But in order to incorporate so many characters, both secondary and peripheral, a large time period needs to be covered and so an 'episodic' structure is frequently the best 'fit' for this type of character.

TIPS: If you want to create an episodic structure for your drama screenplay, think first about the elements of that person's life you want to include in your screenplay (this may be 'easier' with a real person in a biopic than a fictional one, of course). Plot these events on a timeline and work out how they relate to one another. Remember: you don't want these 'episodes' to be random; they need to be 'loosely connected' so your target audience can appreciate the effect the change agent has on other people, which in turn creates that all-important emotional response. So what does your selection of events tell us about a) the change agent, b) the secondary and peripheral characters, and c) the theme or message of the story?

• *Is your character a closed protagonist?* Again, there's absolutely no reason why your closed protagonist cannot be part of a non-linear or episodic structure, but I am going to argue these particular characters flourish best in a linear story. If your character makes a series of bad or self-sabotaging choices (as Miles does in *Sideways*), it often helps to construct the plot in a way that 'adds up' as we go along. The reason for this is because we often become voyeurs to that closed protagonist's bad decision-making, as we might a friend's in 'real life', yet we are absolutely powerless to stop him or her. The story then becomes almost excruciating, as the audience is forced to watch the protagonist 'crash' into his or her realisation. In other cases, like Dumbo, we may invest in that closed protagonist's journey by being 'led' by another character, such as Timothy. Though the story includes the famous 'pink elephants on parade' dream/drunk sequence, I would argue the movie still remains (more or less) linear, because it is Dumbo's story we're essentially following and BOTH he and Timothy are drunk at the same time, leading directly to the moment when both characters realise that Dumbo can fly, when they awake in a tree.

TIPS: If you want us to invest in a character who is his or her own worst enemy, make the audience voyeurs. A linear structure can do this best, irrespective of the time span of the story, though often the shorter, the better: in the case of *Sideways*, just one week. You can also do this by making the audience party to that protagonist's own lies, such as when Miles is woken by his phone ringing at the beginning of the film and tells the caller he's stuck in traffic. We know he's not stuck in traffic, because we're seeing him in bed, hung-over. Alternatively, in the case of such stories as *Dumbo*, the little elephant is constantly misrepresented as stupid, whether it's to the circus-going public, the ringmaster or the other elephants. Dumbo is cast aside and isolated, quite literally unable to speak for himself, and we are asked to feel sorry for him, just as Timothy the mouse does... at first. However, as we get to know Dumbo through Timothy, we stop feeling pity for the little elephant and empathise with his plight instead; a subtle, but huge difference. Dialogue can play a large part in both character and plotting, not only with closed protagonists, but in all drama screenplays.

CASE STUDY 7: THE NON-LINEAR STORY

HOURS (2013)

Writer/Director: Eric Heisserer
Produced by: Peter Safran
Budget: £2.4 million

Q: What's good about it?

A: A powerful metaphor for the struggles ALL parents face, Nolan's journey works on its base level by utilising emotional character work, understated directing and an outstanding central performance from the late Paul Walker.

MY LOGLINE: Newly widowed, a lone father has to keep his premature daughter alive in an incubator in a hospital that has no power and limited supplies due to Hurricane Katrina.

Writing and Selling *Hours*

An LA screenwriter, Eric Heisserer is possibly not the first writer or filmmaker one might think of when it comes to drama screenplays. Known for *A Nightmare on Elm Street* (2010), *The Thing* and *Final Destination 5* (both 2011), Heisserer is a veteran on the Hollywood 'rewrite and reboot' circuit. However, if Heisserer's choice of subject matter for his directorial debut was surprising, so was his choice of star, since Paul Walker is perhaps not the first person many of us might associate with a personal drama, either! Known best for his work in the *Fast & Furious* franchise, Walker had also starred in other movies, most of them comfortably within the genres of thriller and action-adventure, such as *Takers* (2010), *Running Scared* (2006) and *Joy Ride* (2001). Interestingly, Walker was not Heisserer's first choice: 'Paul could play the "swarthy hero", but I wanted an "everyman",' Heisserer explains. 'But our producer had had a good experience working with Paul, so I met with him.' Happily, the two men really hit it off, with Paul convincing Eric he had what it took to play Nolan, the protagonist and new father in *Hours*: 'Paul really wanted it. He had a daughter, Meadow, whom he adored. He knew what fatherhood was about, what the story was about.'

And what is this story about? 'Parenting, specifically fatherhood,' Eric answers, without hesitation. 'There's a lot of stories about motherhood's journey. But from talking to friends, I knew that new fathers often have lots of doubts and anxieties about this huge responsibility they're taking on. I wanted to explore the male psyche.'

Aware Eric does not live in New Orleans or even come from the city, I was keen to ask why he would set his movie there, in the midst of 2005's Hurricane Katrina, and not, say, in the middle of a nameless storm, without the date attached? 'I have friends who live there,' Heisserer says. 'New Orleans is a city that's never forgotten how to celebrate. But when Katrina struck, there were all these stories, these smaller tragedies, that didn't necessarily make the news. One really resonated with me: how doctors and nurses were having to hand-crank generators to keep medical equipment going when the power went out.' So *Hours* comes not from just a single 'place', but several? Eric agrees: 'I believe in what I call "mitosis screenwriting"; I don't make a story from just one I've heard, but many.'

Hours was generally received very well, with Walker's tragic death just a few weeks before the film's release ironically increasing its profile (in fact, it was how I became aware of the movie, in an article 'RIP Paul Walker, Who Was Two Weeks Away from Sharing with Audiences the Finest Performance of His Career' on the blog *Thompson on Hollywood*). *Hours* did inevitably catch some heat from a few (generally younger) critics on the basis of being so markedly different from Walker's previous works. In addition, the distributor took a route that is becoming steadily more common with drama features and sold *Hours* as a thriller, which it most definitely is not. Looking at the poster and DVD box, any moviegoer could be forgiven for thinking it is more in keeping with *Fast & Furious* et al: Walker is looking stressed and rugged, staring into the distance in the midst of skyscrapers and palm trees blowing in the gales; there's even a helicopter flying overhead. 'I understand why distributors make that move,' Heisserer says, 'but I find it disingenuous. I would have preferred for it to be sold as it is, not through deceptive marketing.'

However, in an industry in which commerce is king, creatives rarely get a say in how their own movies are sold to the public and Heisserer was no exception to this. Money was raised the 'traditional' way: with Walker attached, Heisserer was able to generate half the budget needed via foreign pre-sales via its distributor, Voltage. The other half came from what Eric calls 'bonding companies' –

effectively, a big fat (and terrifying) loan. In addition, *Hours* was a punishing shoot; the team had to really hit the ground running. The movie combines a sunken set; fight choreography; water; flares and other fire hazards; a prosthetic baby, plus a real live baby; even a dog. The shoot was for just 18 days, a seemingly impossibly small window for such an ambitious project, but they pulled it off – even though they knew from the outset there would be no opportunity for pick-ups or reshoots. Eric and his team had to get the footage when they got it with no return, meaning effectively a single day's shooting was the equivalent of three days' worth. Eric tells a fantastic story about the scene in which Nolan goes to check on the generator in the basement of the hospital, which is mid-leg deep in murky water. Nolan subsequently gets electrocuted and has to fall back, 'unconscious', into the water. Eric's team only had three identical outfits for Walker for this sequence, so Paul would have to act his electrocution, get dunked, then race out of the water to change, with Wardrobe stripping off his clothes and washing, drying and ironing them, over and over again. Just as the odds are against Nolan in the movie, however, Eric and his team succeeded, in the face of amazing adversity, in getting the film in the can.

My Take on *Hours*

I don't mind admitting when I'm wrong, so I'll say first I was sceptical about *Hours*. I've seen many typecast stars like Walker, both in my career as a script editor and as an avid consumer of movies myself. In my view, the bigger the star, the less likely they are to throw off the 'shackles' of their previous roles and make us believe they are something else entirely. So, before his death, Paul Walker did not figure prominently on my radar, but I'm married to a car nut, so I've watched all the *Fast & Furious* movies multiple times without resentment. I like the soundtracks and the speed and I thought Walker was attractive, but I will be honest and say I thought I was seeing Walker, the actor, as 'the guy who likes to drive fast', not the character, Bryan O'Connor. However, my interest was piqued when I read about *Hours*, so when I saw it on promotion at the supermarket, I bought it. Now, as anyone who knows me in 'real life' realises, I am a phone addict: any movie I watch must compete with Twitter, Facebook and email, whether I am at home watching a DVD, or streaming, or even at the cinema (I realise that makes me some kind of evil heretic, but calm down: I'm usually the only person IN my local, rural cinema). So just like always, I was tapping away as *Hours* began... but my phone was forgotten by the time the short, stylised credit sequence kicked off: I was pulled in straightaway. Within moments, Abigail, in labour and in trouble, is escorted into hospital on a gurney, her husband Nolan holding her hand, telling her it's all going to be okay. But we know it's not going to be okay, and that's why *Hours* makes for such compelling viewing, because it gets worse and worse for Nolan, but, crucially, not in the way we expect.

It would have been very easy to make *Hours* a straight thriller, to set Nolan's struggle to keep his infant daughter alive against a deadline in which a tsunami will arrive when the levee breaks; or to have looters hold him and the baby hostage, 'man-in-the-box-style' like *Buried* (2010) or *Frozen* (also 2010, not to be confused with the 2013 Disney cartoon of the same name!). In the latter, three students – two male, one female – are accidentally left dangling (literally) on a ski lift in freezing temperatures above a closed-down resort. Though Nature is effectively the antagonist in that movie, just as it is in *Hours*, *Frozen* is most definitely a thriller as the students must fight for their lives against the height, the cold and, most notably, man-eating wolves. In contrast, *Hours* is about the private desperation and doubts of a single individual who's not even sure he and his child can both survive the situation and, even if they do, whether he can be a good father. And that's a real strength of *Hours* as far as I'm concerned: the fact baby Abigail (named for her dead mother) is a character in her own right, despite the fact she never speaks a single word (not to mention she is a doll for most of the movie!).

It's important to remember that drama should not automatically equal 'depressing', and the dialogue in *Hours* plays an important part in ensuring the story – which starts with death and destruction – does not become a complete downer. There are genuine moments of warmth whilst Nolan talks to the baby, showing her photographs of her mother and even her own scan photo as he reminisces about how he and Abigail (Snr) came to meet and develop a relationship. There are also moments of humour, such as changing the baby's nappy for the first time, where it looks as if Nolan is performing surgery, or when he discovers that Sherlock, the dog Nolan has to save in the hotel lobby, is supposed to be a rescue dog himself: 'Well, I hope you're embarrassed!' Nolan quips. Yet if *Hours* were a thriller instead, baby Abigail's role in the story would have been quite different: she would have become a problem Nolan had to deal with (thus a prop he would undoubtedly have had to move) as the water got higher; or marauding dogs threatened them; or looters set fire to the building; or all of the above. Instead, against the backdrop of a large-scale disaster, *Hours* is the much smaller, more personal and human tale of a man accepting his role not only as a father, but coming to terms with loss and what it means to be a widower, as well as husband and son.

Though I do not necessarily approve of the distributors' methods of mis-selling *Hours* (which I agree with Eric are deceptive), I do nevertheless have a counter view. Though it's obvious a good portion of those wanting to watch *Hours* on the basis they think it's a thriller will come away disappointed, there must surely be a section of that 'duped' audience who will enjoy the film regardless? I am reminded here of the movie *Stepmom* (1998), starring Julia Roberts, Susan Sarandon and Ed Harris. Sold as a straight comedy, anyone who has actually watched *Stepmom* knows it's the absolutely devastating tale of one mother's journey through terminal cancer (Sarandon). She must not only ready her young children for her death, but also effectively 'train up' her ex-husband's (Harris) new partner (Roberts) to raise them when she has gone. Given the two women are from different generations and outlooks, this leads to huge conflicts, some of them funny, some insightful, others tragic. As a cancer survivor myself, I actively avoid cancer stories. I don't wish to be reminded of what I went through or could have had to face; I even dodge *Holby City* on BBC1. So wild horses could not have made

WRITING AND SELLING DRAMA SCREENPLAYS

me watch *Stepmom* had I not been 'duped' into thinking it was a comedy (with absolutely zero mention of cancer, by the way). Yet I loved *Stepmom* and thought it was authentic and real, with relatable characters. On this basis, I'm willing to bet real money many who came to *Hours* just wanting *Fast & Furious*-type antics still came away with an appreciation for its story and characters in the way I did with *Stepmom*... it's certainly food for thought.

Anyway, I enjoyed *Hours* so much I immediately tweeted Eric Heisserer on a job well done, suggesting my 'Bang2writers' should watch it too. I frequently make movie recommendations, so I didn't think much more about it, until I noticed a reply in my @ box from Heisserer, thanking me. Because I'm the cheeky type, I took the opportunity to ask for his email address, telling him I'd like to ask more details about *Hours*' production. It's something I ask everyone I can on Twitter, so I imagined that would be the end of the exchange, as it has been countless times before. But to my delight Eric replied within minutes and sent me his email address via DM. A few emails later I had the screenplay for *Hours* in my inbox and loaded up to my Kindle, with Eric's challenge to find the differences between the page and what ended up on screen. So here is a round-up:

- **The screenplay itself.** The script for *Hours* is impressively written, furthering the accepted belief that an excellent movie starts on the page. Its format is meticulous and, unlike many US screenplays, it comes in under 100 pages, like a produced British feature script generally would. Being a shooting script by a writer/director, there were inevitably a few instances of camera angles and PUSH ON, etc. but they were not overdone or intrusive. I'm used to reading extremely utilitarian or 'vanilla' scene description, but Eric's showcases his writer's voice, pushes the story forward AND reveals character... yet is lean and visual. The character introductions in the screenplay are a case in point; so often spec screenplays will attempt to introduce characters visually and make the age-old mistake of concentrating on their clothes (especially if they're men) or their looks (especially if they're women). But Heisserer avoids both these obvious traps with ease. Check this out:

> NOLAN HAYES (34, clean-cut white-collar at first glance, cleaned-up blue-collar in truth), talking to SANDRA (30s, focused).

> ABIGAIL LONDON (perhaps 25, perhaps 35, too full of life to gauge).

> Filling out the rest of the table are: MARC (38, gregarious), GLENN (30s, quiet), KAREN (36, coy), Marc's wife, and JEREMY (late 20s and eager) seated next to LUCY (20s, the odd duck).

Spec writers often tell me it is 'impossible' to be both economical with words and visual, but Heisserer proves where the competition is.

- **The dinner party.** Those character intros above take place at a dinner party where Nolan and Abigail (Snr) tell their friends how they met. Yet, as I've already mentioned, the produced version of *Hours* is quite different: Abigail arrives at the hospital on a gurney, already in labour and clearly in difficulties, Nolan holding her hand, telling her everything's gonna be fine, and the dinner party has moved from page one to perhaps 20 minutes in, when Nolan is left alone with baby Abigail in the incubator for the first time. Though I love flashback as a device (in comparison to many script editors and consultants), I have never been a big fan of starting a screenplay or movie with flashback. My main concern has always been, 'Where are we flashing back FROM?' and I believe *Hours* illustrates this issue brilliantly. Eric tells me the dinner party flashback remained at the beginning of the produced movie for much of the editorial process. It was only when the team made the decision to incorporate the stylised credit sequence taking in Hurricane Katrina that they realised they would need to move the dinner party. Why? Think about it: you can't start off with a very intense opening sequence that leads into a happy party; tonally it just does not make sense. Now, the entire movie takes place in the hospital: Nolan arrives with his wife on a gurney, and it ends when he leaves on a gurney and is much more satisfying storytelling as a result.

• *Nolan's arc.* Nolan's arc in both the screenplay and the produced movie is 'textbook' in that he essentially rejects the call of looking after baby Abigail in the first instance with the somewhat cold statement, 'I don't know you,' as he stares down at her tiny form in the incubator. Importantly, however, this rejection does not become what I call 'tick-the-box screenwriting' for, again, Nolan does not do what we expect. We may assume that a grief-stricken man would simply wander out of the hospital in a daze, forgetting his daughter, only for 'something' to happen that makes him turn on his heel and race back to her bedside. But Heisserer sidesteps this predictable beat, having Nolan go down to the hospital morgue instead, searching for his wife's body, finding her on the floor (Hurricane Katrina has meant a surplus of bodies literally piled up in the corridors). What follows is a poignant moment in which he tells Abigail Snr he 'wants her back', making us realise he will do what she would have wanted – look after the baby – but feels completely out of his depth. Unable to exert control over the situation, Nolan grabs a morgue technician to help him move Abigail off the floor and place her inside a body bag. The technician, awkward in the face of Nolan's stark grief, makes a passing comment that 'at least' he has a baby daughter and that her birth is still cause for celebration, further underlining our belief Nolan will go back to baby Abigail, which of course he does. From there, Nolan moves on from saying 'this baby' when he first meets her in the produced version (a line deviation by Paul Walker that was not present in the screenplay) to 'owning' her as 'my daughter' (page 22 in the screenplay and approximately the same in the produced version). As events progress, the dramatic context moves from Nolan doing what he is 'supposed' to do in the first half, to doing 'whatever it takes' in the second, including effectively murdering the looters Jase and Lobo in cold blood to remove the threat they pose before it even really begins. Nolan's arc is completed when his own rescuers give him the crying Abigail on the gurney and he says, smiling this time, 'I know you,' neatly mirroring the first words he said to his child.

- **Nolan the character versus Nolan as Paul Walker plays him.** The lynchpin of *Hours* is Walker's performance, in my opinion. Now, remember, I came to *Hours* quite ambivalent about Walker's acting capabilities, yet I found myself liking Nolan better in the produced movie than the screenplay. I don't dislike Nolan in the screenplay; we root for him and want him to succeed. But Walker breathes life into Nolan and makes him a real person who's quite different from other characters I've seen him play. What's more, Heisserer's directing is understated, so the terrifying and desperate situation Nolan finds himself in never once becomes melodramatic or overly sentimental, even when exhausted Nolan starts to hallucinate and speaks to the 'ghost' of his dead wife, who is wearing her best party dress. This is testament to how movies are a collaborative art. I'm always arguing with writers that a great movie is a sum of all its parts, not just a great screenplay, and *Hours* illustrates this perfectly. Yes, it's great on the page... but it becomes even greater on the screen.

- **Behind the scenes.** Final comparisons between the screenplay on the page and the produced movie are as follows:

  i. **The dog.** It's said filmmakers should 'never work with children or animals' (an adage echoed by Adrian Mead) but, like *Night People*, Heisserer's *Hours* has both. Sherlock the dog is a great addition to the cast; he is involved in some of the stand-out thrilling moments. Sherlock attacks and drives off the first looter, before he can attempt to kill Nolan. However, it's notable that Sherlock is considerably more 'useful' to Nolan on the actual page than he is in the produced movie, with Walker seemingly 'leading' the scenes in which Sherlock appears. When I asked Eric about this, he confessed the dog was a big problem for the team, largely because Sherlock couldn't do even 'half the things he was allegedly trained to do'. As a result, editor Sam Bauer found all the good takes and stitched them together for that performance, leading the rest of the team to joke the dog should receive an award for 'Best Performance by an Editor'!

ii. **The party dress.** The party dress performs an important plot function in that it creates a link between Nolan's hallucination in the 'present' and the flashback to the baby's conception in the 'past'. There's a very notable difference between the screenplay and the produced movie: in the script Abigail Snr's party dress is black, but in the produced movie it is red. Eric tells me that Wardrobe brought out several dresses for the actress playing Abigail, Genesis Rodriguez (*Man on a Ledge* [2012], TV's *Entourage*); Heisserer felt red was more 'alive and loving', especially as, during pre-production, he came up with the concept of making every article or prop that signifies hope in the movie (the Coke cans, flares and emergency bags and so on) red. This notion of red being the 'sign of Nolan's hope' is not present on the page; it is a pure production decision – something screenwriters commonly underestimate. Very often, spec screenwriters think everything they're seeing on screen was on the page, meaning they're not valuing the collaborative element of filmmaking. Yet Eric was the writer as well as the filmmaker of *Hours* – and he did not think of the red motif until pre-production. Fact is, our material may lead a filmmaker to make various creative decisions further down the line, even if that filmmaker is US!

iii. **The baby's conception.** A sex scene is alluded to in *Hours* and could easily have ended up slightly creepy or weird, as Nolan talks to the end result of that lovemaking – baby Abigail herself.

But it's sweet and real, with Nolan having to wait for Abigail Snr as she puts 'that' dress on. Unable to contain himself at the sight of her when she finally reveals her outfit – and she really is gorgeous – they miss their dinner reservations and end up in bed together instead. But rather than being steamy and in danger of becoming cringe-making, Eric's humorous dialogue is in evidence again with Abigail joking, 'That was not like married sex AT ALL,' to which Nolan replies, with a big belly laugh, 'We'd better get dressed before my wife gets back!' Neither of these lines was in the screenplay, as Eric Heisserer explains: 'The post-sex scene was shot on day one of filming and I knew they would be a little awkward together – actors tend to be like that on the first day. They said the lines as written, but it wasn't sounding spontaneous. So I grabbed some 3 x 5 cards and wrote three sets of jokes on them, then gave each of them their lines, without them knowing what their partner's lines were. That way they could be surprised by the joke. When Paul says the line "We'd better get dressed before my wife gets back" and laughs, it's a genuine laugh of him getting the joke.' Sometimes the most authentic, memorable lines are those created on the fly; again, something spec screenwriters underestimate hugely as they obsess over their dialogue on the page.

iv. **The looters' bodies.** In the screenplay, after ambushing and killing Jase and Lobo before they can create an issue for him and baby Abigail, Nolan strings up the bodies on the hospital roof to deter others. Apparently, Heisserer and the team shot this scene and even had it in the edit for a long time, but ultimately felt it raised too many questions, especially considering part of the story's conceit was that Nolan only had between three and four minutes before he needed to hand-crank the generator again: when would he have had time to hang the bodies up? So they scrapped it.

Hours proves a well-written drama screenplay and the subsequent produced movie is about emotional authenticity, strong characterisation and the importance of being open to development ideas and collaboration, not just in getting the words on the page, but the images in the can. Eric Heisserer was able to attract A-list talent to this project that was considerably different from his previous output because of great writing, and because of his commitment to making *Hours* the best it could possibly be, which he recognises was not 100 per cent down to him (as it's not for any filmmaker). As Eric says: 'I've been the first to declare what a great influence Paul was, how his performance elevated the material and made it something more, something better and real... I think it would be rather disappointing if the best version of a movie was its script.'

What We Can Learn from *Hours*

Write Tips:

- Remember Eric's concept of 'mitosis screenwriting' and Gail's notion of two ideas 'smashing together' in her head? Don't mine for ideas for your drama screenplay from just one source; combine pieces of lots of different ones to be in with your best shot of creating a new story that has the most meaning, for the most amount of people.

- Remember the difference between drama and other genres, especially thriller. Dramas are personal struggles, exploring the minutiae of life, such as the male psyche and fatherhood, as in *Hours*. Thrillers have conventions that are quite different.

- Beginning with a flashback invariably does not work; even if it works on the page, it may not work in the edit.

- Remember you can make use of 'textbook' screenwriting techniques like Eric does (such as 'rejecting the call' or a changing from one viewpoint to another in the course of the narrative) without using predictable plotting or characterisation. Never go for what the audience expects, but equally do not bring events or characters completely out of left field, either; fine tune and balance them accordingly.

• Again, moments of warmth and/or humour are absolutely essential if you don't want your drama to be a complete downer. I know I've gone on A LOT about this in the course of this book, but that's because the majority of spec drama screenplays I've seen in the past ten years or so simply don't do this... yet the evidence is right there in front of us: produced drama content NEEDS light and shade!

Selling Points:

• A-list actors often want roles quite different from ones they've played before; so do your research and see if there are any genre stars like Paul Walker who want a change of direction.

• Don't be precious about dialogue. Actors have to say your lines. Sometimes those lines won't seem spontaneous or real because of when they're shot in the schedule, or the actor is having a bad day. So be prepared to come up with solutions, like Eric's jokes on the index cards.

• Be open to the development process and the concept of collaboration, both in pre-production and beyond (if you recall, Gail also makes reference to this in the *Cancer Hair* case study, saying the story continued to evolve in the edit suite). Don't underestimate this process: it can 'elevate the material', as Eric suggests... just remember what YOUR vision is. Don't let too many cooks spoil the broth!

• Distributors may sell your drama feature as something it's not, particularly as a thriller. You most likely won't have any say in this, so roll with any punches you might get from critics about it; it's not worth getting upset over. What's more, it may bring people to your story who enjoy it, but would not have watched it otherwise.

- Difficult shoots often create new opportunities for the story or at least increase camaraderie in the crew, so don't despair if the production of your drama screenplay goes awry. It's all material!

WHATEVER IT TAKES

'BUT IT'S A TALKY FILM'

Most script readers, producers and agents will agree the average spec screenplay has too much dialogue in it. Yet the average spec screenwriter takes very little notice of this proclamation, believing their craft or their individual screenplay to be the exception to the rule! It's not difficult to see the thought process behind this: after all, they work hard on differentiating their characters' voices and on writing great lines actors would LOVE to say aloud, so they're home free, right? Again: a million times, NO. Your screenplay is NOT the exception to any supposed 'rules', especially if it is a drama screenplay! In the case of genre screenplays like horror, thriller, or even comedy, many scribes accept that characters must 'earn the right to speak' and often try to relate dialogue to both character motivation and plot. This frequently goes out of the window, however, when the same writers attempt to write drama, the most oft-cited reason being, 'But it's a talky film!'

Again, it's not difficult to see why spec drama writers feel this way. It's definitely true that dialogue plays a (slightly) larger part in drama screenplays than genre. What's more, it can even be a selling point 'off the page', especially when it comes to the likes of acclaimed drama writers such as Aaron Sorkin. If we consider a produced drama like *The Social Network* (2010), the story of social media phenomenon Facebook, it is clear that witty dialogue is a 'high point' of the movie. Being a relatively recent true story that has been widely reported, we think we 'know' how it will work out for all the characters involved (Zuckerberg squeezes his co-founder Eduardo Saverin out and Facebook takes over the world), just like we think we 'know' how it will work out in *Saving Mr Banks*. In addition, Zuckerberg (and indeed most of the characters) are hard to relate to, being so privileged and, ultimately, dislikeable. It's perhaps part of the human condition to admire those who can do what we cannot; but, equally, many of us also want to crush others like bugs if they're 'too clever' and/or have superiority complexes... Mark Z and friends have such superiority complexes in abundance, which is probably the principal reason nerds are so reviled (rightly or wrongly) in high school and the world at large. So, we can see Sorkin's dilemma: how can he make his audience LIKE such ultimately dislikeable people? The answer is simple: make them funny! Generally in life, IF you're funny – and a male, preferably white – you get a free pass to be as obnoxious as you like. Sorkin does this with aplomb in *The Social Network*, getting the audience on board regardless of what the characters actually do! This combination of funny dialogue and despicable actions means the audience ends up in a curious place, hating AND admiring the characters at the same time. No mean feat.

But there's an obvious mega-difference between a Sorkin screenplay and the average drama screenplay dialogue. The latter's is just NOT GOOD, regardless of how hard a writer has worked to differentiate characters' voices, or write the so-called 'great lines'. The main issue is down to the fact writers appear to think spec drama screenplays are ultimately theatrical in nature; they end up writing what I call 'screenPLAYS'. In other words, writers think drama screenplays equal people standing or sitting around, simply talking. As a result, screenplays will become long chains of exchanges, going on for pages and pages, occasionally broken up by a line or two of scene description to promote the idea of 'movement' in the scene. But it is a lie: there is no real movement in the scene. Often that scene description is just 'filler': staring out a window; a raised eyebrow; a shake of the head. Readers won't fall for it and neither should writers. Screenwriting is a visual medium; we all know this. Yet many spec screenplays contain very few visuals at all, with drama screenplays being the biggest culprit in this respect. But how do writers tackle this and turn their drama screenPLAY around?

REMEMBER, SCREENPLAY

Sometimes, an obvious problem like your drama screenplay being 'too theatrical' thanks to its having 'too much dialogue' requires an obvious solution: writers need to think SCREENplay, not screenPLAY. But what does this entail? How about this, for starters:

- *Cut, cut, cut.* Very often, spec drama screenplay characters will make long 'speeches' every single time they speak: typically four or five lines, or even more. Writers make this mistake because they realise correctly that drama is about eliciting an emotional response... but instead of trying to elicit emotion from their target audience, they attempt to do this with their characters instead! As a result, their drama screenplay becomes very melodramatic, with characters naming their pain and splurging their FEELINGS OF WOE all over the place. UGH! Get rid. Same goes for other extremes of emotion, especially anger, but also other stuff like romance. Think about the people in your life: do they say exactly what they mean all the time? Of course not. Loads of things get in the way of 'true' honesty. During our ENTIRE LIVES, we can probably count the number of times anyone is truly honest with us on one hand, yet here is a screenplay full of this stuff? Readers can't believe in the story or your characters as a result.

  TIPS: So, if you want us to believe, make it DIFFICULT for your characters to say what they truly mean. Do it any way you want. But do it.

- *It's about character behaviour, NOT talking.* An old screenwriting adage is 'characters are not what they SAY, but what they DO.'

Many Bang2writers over the years have confessed they're 'not really sure' what this means, usually because they feel that if they can't have their characters saying what they need or want, their motivation is 'unclear'. The key word, however, is 'do', as in 'behaviour'. We know people want various things from us in 'real life' by the behaviour they exhibit, even if they don't actually speak it aloud. The most obvious example would be romantic relationships. If you're British like me, you'll know dating can be a minefield because very few of us will come right out and say we want to go out with someone! Yet most of us pair up at least a few times in our lives and this is because we decode what that other person DOES. Sometimes it's obvious (i.e. s/he sends us a signed Valentine's card, or takes the opportunity to plant a snog on us under the mistletoe at the office Christmas party)... sometimes it's NOT so obvious (i.e. s/he hangs out at the photocopier in the hope of talking, making you think, 'Hmmm, does s/he do that to avoid working, or to talk to me??'). Misunderstandings, threats and opportunities will abound in our real, lived experiences of romance and its pitfalls, so these lived experiences must help 'inform' our characters' actions in our drama screenplays, for them to be authentic.

TIPS: Think about your characters' motivations or goals in your drama screenplay. Do you have any direct experience of the same? Great! Make a list of the events that happened, the people involved and what they did, both for you and/or against you, plus your own response. Now try and imagine WHY they might have taken the course of action they did and HOW you could have reacted instead? Try putting yourself in their shoes, even if it pisses you off (arguably, it's good if it does, you might learn something extra!). But if you don't have any direct experience, that's okay: find people who have real experiences of what you want to write about. You can do this in 'real life' or you can read interviews with people, but DON'T rely on just one account; remember Eric and Gail's 'mitosis screenwriting'. Again, make lists of what people DO and why you think they followed that path. That's what 'write what you know' ultimately means; it doesn't mean you have to have lived it personally – just do your research!

- **Substitute visuals for dialogue.** Remember: most scenes in drama screenplays are STATIC, with characters talking about 'whatever', with the screenwriter sneaking in the odd line of description here or there to describe someone doing something PHYSICAL, e.g. crying, putting a hand on someone's shoulder, hugging them, etc. YAWN. You need to know how to make scenes VISUAL. Watching a play, we will sit in the audience and stare at the characters moving around on stage; that's it. Movies are different: the various camera shots and transitions (wide shot, close-up, POV, dissolve, match cut, etc.) can make the audience feel they are 'right there' with the characters, sometimes even looking directly through THEIR EYES. Never lose sight of the fact that you should be using visuals WHEREVER POSSIBLE, because 'scene description is scene action,' as *Script Secrets'* Bill Martell says in his fantastic '16 Steps to Better Scene Description', which is probably the 'how to' article I've recommended most to Bang2writers in the last ten years or so.

TIPS: The purpose of drawing your attention back to the mechanics of filmmaking is NOT to say you should include camera shots and transitions in your spec drama screenplay (generally speaking, you should NOT). Instead, think of how the finished film will look, then render that as 'image' (aka scene description) on the page in such a way that we can appreciate the world view and internal conflict of the characters. Again, there are no 'rules' on how to do this, but if you find yourself stuck, watch those produced dramas you feel have done it well (and read their screenplays!) and take a note of HOW they did it. At first, you may find yourself copying, but keep going! As 'rendering as image' via scene description 'clicks' in your head, you will develop your own style.

- *Man the perimeters!* Most spec drama writers do not give themselves an effective 'perimeter' for scenes, preferring instead for the scene to go on for as long as it 'feels right'. As a result, too many scenes end up way too long, often because they end up feeling 'bloated' with dialogue (or, up until three or four years ago, because those scenes were 'bloated' with scene description! Always interesting to see how writing habits and mistakes change, en masse, in the spec pile). Writers need to challenge themselves to ensure each individual scene is as dramatic as it can be; or, as another old screenwriting adage goes, they need to 'enter late and leave early'.

  TIPS: I frequently suggest spec writers have 'up to a page' for 'ordinary' scenes and 'up to three pages' for 'extraordinary' scenes in genre screenplays. Obviously that's not set in stone and, in the case of drama screenplays, there's perhaps a little more leeway for 'extra' dialogue, though those dreaded chains of exchanges must never take priority over a drama script's visual potential. Think very carefully about scene length and its impact on your story and the characters; never just leave it to chance.

- *Dialogue is an ILLUSION.* Very often spec drama writers will look at produced writers 'known' for their dialogue, like the aforementioned Sorkin, and believe the success of the work is down to that great dialogue alone. But it's important to remember not only that the produced writer may have more 'leeway' than a spec writer, but that Sorkin doesn't just write 'good dialogue'; he is the WHOLE PACKAGE. In a world in which there are more spec screenplays than anyone could ever want, the reason Sorkin has a career and Joe X doesn't is because Sorkin can do ALL OF IT: story, character, dialogue, visuals, THE WORKS.

  TIPS: Don't 'work on' your craft, then; INVEST in it. Do you even know what you need to invest in – what are your weak points? How do they compare to your strengths? If you don't know, why not?

If you do know, what are you doing about it? And by when? You need to be the whole package, too, and you need to be it ASAP or you might as well go home. You have to be willing to challenge your writing to be the best it can possibly be, otherwise it doesn't matter how great you are at selling yourself: the screenplay will let you down and you won't see others for dust. With this in mind, then, it's time for our final case study – a drama screenplay still in development, just like yours, and how its writer/director plans to get it made, whatever it takes... just like you!

CASE STUDY 8: THE GUERILLA FILMMAKER

ROCKETBOY

Writer/Director: Chris Jones
Produced by: Judy Goldberg
Budget: Unproduced (so far!)

Q: What's good about it?

A: In a corner of the market overtaken by both American Media Imperialism and animation via the likes of Pixar, DreamWorks and Disney, *Rocketboy* offers a rare chance for family audiences to glimpse a decidedly 'British' 1960s story world in which the Great Outdoors meant adventure, summers were never-ending and friendships felt like they would last forever.

<u>MY LOGLINE:</u> An old man recounts his childhood building rockets with his grandfather in the 1960s, detailing how he fell in love along the way.

Writing and Selling *Rocketboy*

This case study is slightly different, because the movie is as yet unproduced (the only reason I would ever obey the 'no spoilers' rule, in fact!). What's more, no book on taking your filmmaking destiny in your own hands would be complete without a word from the original Guerrilla Filmmaker, Chris Jones. Known for his stirring 'Do It Yourself' books and classes, and working out of the iconic Ealing Studios, Chris is also director of the London Screenwriters' Festival, overseeing the rest of its many classes year round. But in an industry in which trainers often haven't actually done what they teach, Chris has: he practises what he preaches. He's written screenplays, raised finance, plus made and sold the films... and in the case of LondonSWF's *50 Kisses* initiative, even crowdsourced them and got them in the *Guinness Book of Records*! So I was only too happy to give Chris notes on the two projects currently in development with Living Spirit, his filmmaking arm: one, a horror called *Transplant*, was an intriguing tale about playing God, which I liked a great deal, but felt (at that time) to still need work. However, it was the other script, a family drama called *Rocketboy*, that really caught my attention and fired up my own imagination.

Including a family drama AGAIN may seem like a strange choice at first glance (but then this has become a recurring theme in this book). But many family dramas include elements of comedy or action-adventure, surely taking them beyond the 'usual' remit for a drama story? No, says Chris: 'Family drama is not about being the fastest, or getting the girl/boy, or winning the game... it's about taking a stand for what you believe, and then acting with courage for that belief. And core to this is that kids MUST know that failure is always a possibility. I feel many stories are afraid of upsetting kids, not remembering all the great ones had real jeopardy, consequence and often loss.' I totally agree with Chris. When I consider the movies that made the most impression on me as a young child, the list reads like a Muppet/Puppet Appreciation Society: *The Dark Crystal* (1982), a tale of how everyone has the potential to do both evil and good, so tolerance and understanding are a must; *Labyrinth* (1986), a story of how family ties matter more than sibling rivalry; and *The NeverEnding Story* (1984), a dark and epic journey of self-actualisation via the power of the imagination. Interestingly, all of these movies are quest narratives drawing on Homer's *Odyssey*, in which their protagonists are tested and even betrayed in the course of the story, facing heartbreak and loss. As Chris points out: 'I believe kids are robust and hungry for experience they can relate to, stories they can grow from... the playground is a battlefield!'

An emotional response is absolutely key to most family dramas. Also, like many produced dramas destined for more adult audiences, family films frequently mine those six themes I identify in the course of this book: 'joy' is the most obvious, but even devastation, on occasion. After all, what adult now, growing up in the eighties, can forget Atreyu's horse, Artax, succumbing to the Swamp of Sadness in *The NeverEnding Story*? But it's a family movie more recent that is *Rocketboy*'s biggest influence: Disney's *Bridge to Terabithia*, the story of two opposites, a country boy and a city girl, who create a fantasy world of trolls, monsters, ogres and giants, which they rule over together as king and queen. 'I wanted to capture those first moments when we, as young people, fall deliriously in love, even if the experience is confusing, scary and overwhelming,' says Chris. 'It's a love letter back to my former self.' But, most importantly perhaps, family dramas frequently have messages for their young audiences, moral or otherwise, that adults can also relate to. Yet that doesn't have to mean being preachy with it, Chris argues: 'Kids are small adults and really sharp as tacks. Let them live emotionally challenging experience through drama, so they feel informed about who they would like to be when similar problems manifest in their own lives... inspire them to be the most courageous they can be.' But how does a writer 'capture' emotion, so this might be transferred to their target audience, via storytelling?

When I think of the two family dramas that have elicited a strong emotional response in me recently, the first that leaps out immediately is *Frozen* (2013). As the highest-grossing animated movie ever, Disney's *Frozen* needs little introduction; it is a retelling of the classic ice queen fairy tale and contains not one but two three-dimensional female characters. Elsa and Anna are princesses and sisters, with one's 'gift' (or 'curse') coming between them, isolating them from each other as they grow up. Elsa's ability to create ice is seen by some as a metaphor for being gay; others as being symbolic of mental health issues, disability or other things that may make a teenager socially 'awkward', in comparison to the bubbly, lonely (but otherwise 'normal') sister, Anna. But it is not Elsa's story: it is Anna who must recognise her sister's right to be whoever she needs to be... only then can Anna truly be there for her. One of the things Disney does especially well in my opinion is relating their stories to girls in the audience, so I was gratified when my little girl, just seven years old, quipped, 'I feel very emotional right now!' as we were leaving the cinema.

The second family drama that left a lasting impression by eliciting that all-important emotional response in me was *Epic*, also 2013. Despite its rather poor title, *Epic* is the story, not only of the importance of being environmentally friendly, but of how to cope with grief. After the loss of her mother, city girl Mary Katherine (MK) goes to live in the countryside with her eccentric and estranged botanist father, who insists there are little people called 'Leafmen' in the woods. Of course, MK's father is correct and she finds herself caught up in the little people's war with the Boglins, putrefying creatures symbolic of deforestation and pollution. Strikingly, *Epic* features a female protagonist who is a teen, rather than 'tween' (ten to twelve years old). This is not only very unusual in family dramas (teens are frequently cast in the antagonist's role, especially as the older brother or sister), but forms part of the moral message of duty and sacrifice that underscores the whole movie. When Queen Tara of the Leafmen is mortally wounded by the Boglins, she passes the role of finding her successor on to MK, who happens to be present. Tara explains she realises MK doesn't know what her place is in their world, but that everything is connected and she must do this quest for Tara, so the balance of both their worlds can be preserved. This is a brilliant piece of writing, because very often teenagers are not sure of who they are, or what their place in the world is. As a result, they may underestimate how everything and everyone is connected, which can lead to conflict between them and other people, especially figures of authority like parents and teachers, who usually have their best interests at heart. Here, then, in Epic, is a way of ensuring older kids have that same chance Chris describes of 'living through drama' so they too can become 'courageous', just as MK has to be in the course of the quest against the evil Boglins.

American titans like Disney, Pixar, DreamWorks and, to a lesser extent, Blue Sky (which produced *Epic*) have cornered the market. But, unlike *Epic* or *Frozen*, *Rocketboy* is not an animated film. Also, Chris and his team are not as heavily financed as Disney, which made *Bridge to Terabithia* for a budget of about $30 million. That may be chump change to Hollywood, but is a figure out of the grasp of most indie filmmakers, especially British ones. 'I don't plan to compete, just to make the best movie I can,' Chris explains. 'When I get to distribution I will assess the market at that time and make choices based on the landscape then, not now. What I can tell you is that it's better to sidestep the bull in the bull fight, with effortless grace, than it is to directly engage the bull head on.' So, with its large cast, plus its larger-than-life arena that includes an entire rural off-shore island (complete with lighthouse!), not to mention its period setting in the 1960s and stunts involving actual rockets and children in the water in capsized dinghies, how on earth does Chris hope to get this film funded?! 'We are living in a massive evolution for all creative industries,' Chris replies. 'There's always money for the right project... we will find money from the traditional sources such as the Enterprise Investment Scheme (tax relief), broadcasters, but also new tools and ideas and, of course, the crowd.' It's so easy to talk down such plans and dismiss them as pipe dreams. But Chris's enthusiasm calls to mind Alison Owen and Kelly Marcel on *Saving Mr Banks*. Some might have called the women 'crazy' for even considering potentially 'wasting their time' on a project that could so easily have faltered, had Disney not come on board. Yet *Saving Mr Banks* now exists, proving perhaps you have to be both passionate about your project AND ambitious to be in with a chance of making something of worth. I have faith *Rocketboy* will come into being on the same basis.

Write Tips:

- Family drama isn't about 'just' winning or losing, but taking a stand for what you believe in, so they often involve sporting contests or 'battles' of some kind against figures of authority, especially parents, teachers, nasty neighbours or baddie businessmen. Often such battles are metaphorical, with the target of the child protagonist's resentment completely unaware of how s/he is seen. In the case of *Bridge to Terabithia*, Jess casts his father as the antagonist and they can only find their way back to each other after a tragedy, 'seeing' each other for the first time in years. In the best family dramas, there is a very real sense of jeopardy and potential loss: the days of 'it was all a dream', where characters can just 'wake up' Alice in Wonderland-style, is no more tolerated by children than it is adults!

- Though many family dramas stray into realms of fantasy, science fiction and/or action-adventure, many, such as *Bridge to Terabithia* and *Rocketboy*, create world views from a child's POV, giving us a glimpse of how their psyche works, rather than being 'event-driven'. Family dramas are most typically in the 'Joy' subtype, but frequently include elements of 'Wonder' and 'Bittersweet', as well as 'Devastation', which *Bridge to Terabithia* does brilliantly with Leslie's shock death. Family dramas infrequently use 'Shock and Awe', since this most often takes the characters into action-adventure and event-driven, rather than character-driven, storytelling, but not always.

- Family dramas often rely on the quest as a metaphor for growing up, especially in the case of 'coming of age' dramas. As Chris suggests, children and teens can 'grow' via drama; they're making sense of the world around them. So how can you relate your story to this concept? What did your childhood mean to you? To other people you grew up with? To those you don't know? What would you tell yourself 'back then' that you know now? Ask everyone.

Selling Points:

- Family drama is an underrated opportunity to use various methods of storytelling, arenas, symbolism and allusion to disseminate a complex message to an eclectic group of people, both young and old. In my experience, there are relatively few family dramas in the spec pile and almost all of them are American, which I always find interesting. British and European children have relatively little to watch that originates in their home countries in comparison to their American counterparts, and whilst it is difficult going up against the 'Big Three' (Disney, Pixar, DreamWorks) and other large animation studios, as I've already said multiple times, the more difficult path is often the most worthwhile. Plus, as Chris points out – don't compete, sidestep instead! There's room for everyone if you play it 'right'.

- Enabling children in the audience to link stories and relate them to one another, so they can 'live through drama', as Chris suggests, is a smart move. Children are more media literate than they have ever been, so if they can work out hidden meanings in your story, you will keep their attention longer. What's more, parents love their kids learning stuff in their leisure time, so get parents on board and you're likely to sell tickets or DVDs, because it's adults who hold the purse strings.

- Everyone has a favourite family drama from when they were a child – and I mean everyone! Reference them, pay homage to them or update them (without doing an out-and-out adaptation) and you may find this a great way of getting other people on board with you.

- Make decisions based on what is going on at the time. The industry is constantly in flux, so you can't plan for every minute eventuality in advance. Every film is essentially a leap of faith, but you can make that leap 'shorter' by knowing how the industry works and what opportunities are available to you, such as tax breaks.

There is always money for the 'right' project. Lots of writers and filmmakers don't believe this, but there are always ways of making it happen for your drama screenplay if you're determined enough and willing to go the long haul.

And remember...

Ambition is great, but passion is key. None of the dramas in this book were 'easy' to pull off. Most productions are not easy in truth, but, as mentioned, you may at least have a starting point or ballpark for genre. So if you're hoping that someone will come along and just take your drama screenplay off your hands and make it, you should probably write something else. Seriously. But if you can throw yourself into this story; research it; challenge yourself; write and rewrite times infinity; plus stick with it NO MATTER WHAT *and* find others who will commit to doing the same, you might just have a produced drama, about ten or twenty years from now! So I'll wait for my invite to the Oscars, Golden Globes and BAFTAs... See you there!

WRITING AND SELLING YOUR OWN SPEC DRAMA SCREENPLAY

A NEW B2W RESOURCE

As mentioned in this book copious times, far too many spec drama screenplays are simply 'movies of movies' and lack emotional truth, thus failing to connect with the industry pro they are targeting. Scribes often believe 'drama = depressing' and thus recycle tired tropes and clichés ad nauseam, failing to grasp that the best drama screenplays offer myriad personal POVs and emotional stories about struggling through life and its many inspiring, wonderful and/ or devastating challenges. With this in mind, then, I have created a new resource* to walk you through not only writing your own spec drama screenplay, but finishing it and getting it 'out there', to the people who matter to you in your own filmmaking journey.

You will find a copy of this resource to download to your desktop on the Kamera Books website at kamerabooks.co.uk/resources

Elements you must consider in advance of writing include (but are not limited to):

- **WHAT** is this story?
- **WHO** is it for?
- **WHY** does your project stand out?

- **WHERE** do you want to send it?
- **WHEN** do you want it done by?

First, though, a warning: this resource is NOT something you can simply fill in over the course of a single afternoon; it will require mulling over for a matter of weeks, minimum. Dig deep into your psyche, be brave, tell the truth to YOURSELF about what matters to you… and that all-important story, its characters and its audience will follow. Good luck!

NAME & CONTACT DETAILS

You may end up using this document (or a version of it) to interest others in your project – why not? – but, if you do, NEVER forget to put your contact details, including your email address, on it. Documents get moved around from folder to folder, Dropbox to Dropbox by industry pros, and who-sent-what gets forgotten. So never let them forget you or your work!

WORKING TITLE

Remember: always check out titles on the likes of IMDb, try them out on friends, social media, etc. Do not go with the first thing that enters your head! A drama should not sound like a thriller or horror, for example; dramas typically are atmospheric, or use main character or place names. Avoid very odd-sounding titles, the names of iconic movies (or similar) and avoid song titles (there are soooo many in the spec pile!).

PREMISE AND LOGLINE

- What is my idea?
- Why this story?
- What existing stories are 'like' my idea?

- How do these existing stories differ?
- What overriding type of drama story is this? (Joy, Devastation, Wonder, etc.) And why?
- What is the story world and how does it inform the story?
- What is my theme/message? (Do I have one?)
- Why do I need to tell this story? What would happen if I didn't?
- Who are my characters (names, ages, relationships, etc.)?
- What types of characters are they?
- Why NOW in their lives?
- How will I ensure authenticity?
- What type of structure do I want to use in this story?

LENGTH

Be honest with yourself. Are you running before you can walk? Writing a great drama is DIFFICULT. It's better to write a brilliant short drama film, and find people to get it made, than to end up writing and rewriting a drama feature screenplay that stays on your desktop forever.

TARGET AUDIENCE

- Who is the audience for this story?
- What projects 'like mine' has this audience liked before?
- How is my project different to the above?
- What do they get out of it?
- How can I ensure there is emotional truth?
- How would an audience relate to the characters' world views here?
- Why would they want to?

OUTLINE

- *The characters* – not just their biographies, but what they WANT and NEED (not always the same thing!). Your protagonist and antagonist may be at odds, but in drama they may be the same person; your secondaries need a strong reason to help or hinder your main characters in their goal/s too.

- **The story structure** – whether you use three acts, 'Save the Cat', the 22 Steps, the mini-movie method, non-linearity or something else, your audience needs to be able to follow the story to invest in your characters' journey. Put the work in at foundation level, by whatever means necessary!

- **The plot beats** – especially the beginning, middle and end. This document is for you to work out how this story goes from A to B to C, so the writing of your actual draft goes as smoothly as possible. You're not setting the plot in stone. You may end up deviating from this outline and that's fine; it is just a starting point!

- **This outline is as long as it needs to be** – you can write a polished one-pager and/or treatment LATER.

STATEMENT OF INTENT

This is a 'note to self', if you like, on WHY you're writing this project and HOW you're going to make it happen, whether the piece ends up physically produced or not!

- What do I care about?
- How do I see the world?
- Why do I want to explore this subject/person, etc.?
- Why is it important I share this with the world?
- What are my goals i) short term, ii) long term?
- What drives me in these directions? Why?
- Within what timescale do I want to achieve the above, i) ideally, or ii) in the worst case scenario?
- If i), what would I do after that? If ii), what would I do during this time period as well to keep 'on track'?

FINDING COLLABORATORS

- Who do I already know who might be interested?
- Why would others want to tell this story with me?
- Who has made films like mine?
- Who might want to make films like mine?
- Where would I find them?
- How can I make new contacts?
- How can I persuade others I know what I'm talking about?

MONEY

- What are the opportunities for this story?
- What are the threats?
- What is the budget for this story, ideally? Realistically?
- How does the budget affect what I can do (i.e. portmanteau)?
- What can I use that's FREE to create a buzz about myself and/ or my project?
- Are there new ways I can approach this story (transmedia, *50 Kisses*)?

GETTING STARTED *NOW*!

- WHAT do I need to make this a reality?
- What skills base do I already have?
- What knowledge gaps do I have?
- What are my writing weaknesses?
- What are my own potential issues or flaws?
- What actionable steps can I take to begin this journey?
- What can I do TODAY?
- When will I FINISH WRITING and 'sign off' on a draft?

SWOT ANALYSIS

This is a consolidation of the questions you've already answered in the course of this document. You should know now WHAT your project is, WHO it is for, WHY it stands out, WHERE you would want to send it, and WHEN you want it done by, as well as a multitude of other very important elements! Don't just start writing; give your spec drama screenplay its very best chance of a) being brilliant, and b) getting some attention out there in the marketplace/with industry pros. Good luck!

STRENGTHS	WEAKNESSES
OPPORTUNITIES	THREATS

ADDENDUM

So, you've read the case studies on how other people have navigated their way through the writing and selling of their drama screenplays. You've scoured the various screenwriting tips I've outlined here for your screenplay, as well as pitching it and presenting yourself. You've taken on board my warnings about what not to do, as well as a brief history of drama movies: the difference between 'devastation' and 'depressing'; internal versus external conflict; what audiences do and don't like; and how it's possible to still screw up, no matter how careful you are! In other words, you realise writing and selling a drama screenplay is a hugely difficult journey to make, even for those scripts with major stars attached; or for producers, writers and directors with a track record. I wouldn't blame you for thinking it appears a Sisyphean task! *What is the point*, you might ask, *if writers like Kelly Marcel or Eric Heisserer, with Hollywood screenwriting résumés to die for, have it so hard? I might as well not even bother! I must surely have triple the distance to cover?*

But here's the good news: you DON'T have triple the distance! This is the thing: when it comes to drama, EVERYONE has the same ground to cover. It's fraught with frustration and peril (and there's probably a giant scorpion at the end of the world as well like the ancient Greeks believed!), but if you're willing to put in the hours and keep going, you WILL get there. But to do this, there are five things you must do:

1. **DARE!** Effective drama can literally be about anything and anyone, in any form you like. You may decide drama feature screenwriting and filmmaking is not for you; perhaps you prefer the idea of short film, web series, television or transmedia? Delivery is not important when it comes to real drama: the medium is the message and vice versa. Instead, concentrate on the story and your characters, but most of all, DARE to be different. Remember *Blue Valentine* and how it took ten years to make it to production and distribution, even with significant box-office draws like Michelle Williams and Ryan Gosling attached? On paper, *Blue Valentine* is a hugely hard sell. A non-linear tragedy about a marriage break-up?? Yikes, talk about a downer! – yet huge stars were attracted to this material, simply because it was so well written. Their faith, which made them stay with the project and its multiple rewrites for over a decade, was well founded, too: *Blue Valentine* won several awards and accolades, setting writer/director Derek Cianfrance up for his next movie, *The Place Beyond the Pines* (2012), another drama with an all-star cast. So whether you want to write a movie that realistically only ONE studio such as Disney can make, as with *Saving Mr Banks* (2013); or a drama involving disability like *Dear Frankie* (2004); or an ambitious portmanteau movie like *Night People* (2005); or you want to take on the likes of giants like Pixar with a (non-animated) movie for children like the as-yet-unproduced *Rocketboy*, you simply must go for it! DON'T try and play it safe, thinking you have more 'chance' of getting produced that way, because you do not. If you want others to get on board with you, you MUST be daring. It's the only chance of getting your bravery rewarded.

2. **Banish all clichés.** Whatever story you want to tell, whatever character you conceive of, they simply MUST NOT be 'the usual'. In drama territory, the usual clichés might be sinkhole estates, teenage mums and drug dealer boyfriends, but just because your story does not feature any of these elements doesn't mean you're off the hook! You must identify not only the story you want to

tell and its characters, but also the TYPE, such as 'Devastation', 'Shock and Awe', 'Bittersweet', 'Hope/Joy' or 'Gratitude'. You must watch all the predecessors in your story's category, plus you must be able to pinpoint your own story's theme, whether it's a shocking tale about morality, or a bittersweet 'Anti Rom' or 'Dramedy' (or something else!). Your characters must present refreshing and genuine world views that defy stereotyping and well-mined tropes, but which, at the same time, are not too far out of left field either. Remember the likes of *Juno*, a credible and intriguing portrait of a teenage girl who becomes pregnant, who is never once sexualised or 'ruined'? Or Olive in *Little Miss Sunshine*, a child and free spirit, who inspires all the adults around her?

3. ***Tell the truth.*** Remember the essence of drama is not that dreaded 'd' word: 'depressing'! Instead, drama is about struggle, the psyche and internal, rather than external, conflict. Audiences want to be involved in the emotions of your central character and his or her world view. People will get on board with your storytelling and your characters' journeys if they feel they are authentic. This means your story can even change people's minds altogether! Remember how much I *didn't* want to read Gail Hackston's *Cancer Hair*? Or how I would have avoided *Stepmom*, starring Susan Sarandon and Julia Roberts, had I known in advance it dealt with a terminal diagnosis? Yet I couldn't take my eyes away from either of these stories, because they both told the truth in a way I could invest in. The stories you tell don't even need to be YOUR stories for you to do this either (though it can obviously help). Even if it is your story, it never hurts to ask for multiple points of view to help inform those of your characters. Just remember to stay on track with regard to what you first conceived and why, to avoid going off at a tangent.

4. ***Be adaptable... but don't sell out.*** Sometimes an Industry Pro might like your idea, but want to change it. Sometimes it will be for the obvious better. For example, if you conceive of your drama screenplay as a 60-minute TV drama, yet a producer wants to

make it as a 90-minute feature with a great, bankable star in the lead instead, then why the hell not?? Other times, that Industry Pro will have a different idea of what your material means and their suggestions will not be good. Don't be afraid of holding on to your screenplay in these situations, rather than signing it away regardless. If one Industry Pro likes your writing, trust me: *another will*. Yet over the years I've heard multiple writers express doubts about 'being on the same page' as a producer or filmmaker, yet signing anyway... only to live to regret it! If you genuinely think the Industry Pro doesn't 'get' what your story is about, listen to me: walk away. Do NOT work on the basis that a bird in the hand is worth two in the bush, because YOU are the bush! I'll explain why, next.

5. *Understand the emphasis is on YOU to get this done.* This is the truth: unless your fantastic drama screenplay is an adaptation of a bestseller you happen to have the rights to, NO ONE is going to come looking for it, no matter how well written it is. This isn't because The Industry hates drama, or great storytelling, or gifted filmmakers, but because The Industry is risk-averse financially. That's just the way it is; we can fight that – and lose! – or build this into our plans and expectations. Talk about a no-brainer! So, if you want to write a brilliant drama screenplay that is daring and tells the truth about well-conceived, non-clichéd characters, know that there are two routes available to you in 'selling' it:

   a. *'Off the page'.* This means you're using your brilliant drama screenplay to sell YOURSELF and your writing ability, in order to get paid work on other people's ideas. There's nothing wrong with this and many professional writers have received their big break off the back of a great sample drama screenplay, especially in television. Just know the market is flooded with people just like you, doing the same thing; plus it takes YEARS, not months, of repeated submissions, networking and follow ups to 'make it'. You have to keep your feet on the ground.

There is no alternative and no short cut. That's the bad news... again, the good news is, keep going and how can you NOT get somewhere eventually? Another no-brainer.

b. **Do it yourself.** It's a reality that studios and networks are favouring genre screenplays and movies at the moment, so by wanting to write a drama screenplay you are literally swimming AGAINST the tide. Generally speaking, in The Industry, if you want to break the rules, you'll need to take the risks by making the movie yourself. That's not to say you won't find any investors: remember the producer Cassian Elwes, who got *Dallas Buyers Club* funded on the basis of previous favours owed, rather than its concept? Or Eric Heisserer, who managed to finance *Hours* on the basis that a European distributor picked it up before shooting, because it starred Paul Walker? But be realistic, too: know that making a drama screenplay and getting it out there will be difficult; more difficult than making a slasher horror or gross-out comedy. But then, as the twenty-sixth president of the USA, Theodore 'Teddy' Roosevelt, said:

> Nothing in the world is worth having or worth doing unless it means effort, pain, difficulty... I have never in my life envied a human being who led an easy life. I have envied a great many people who led difficult lives and led them well.

Dallas Buyers Club might have been the 'most stalled screenplay' for the best part of 20 years, but what do you suppose Cassian Elwes's peers think of its Oscar-winning glory now? *Hours* may not have received quite the same accolades in terms of statuettes, but as one of Paul Walker's last films it is both a fitting testimony to the late star's acting skills and a showcase for Eric Heisserer's ability to turn around a previously typecast actor's persona!

So BE that object of envy. Tread the more difficult path of the drama screenplay... *and do it well!* Good luck!

RESOURCES

FIRST, A 'THANK YOU'

I have tried to list as many writers' resources and useful sites as possible but will inevitably forget some, so first of all: thanks to all the writers, publishers, filmmakers, script consultants, competitions, services, trainers, readers, agents and assistants who endeavour to share their insights on the web with students of the craft. We salute you! It can seem like a thankless task sometimes, but you are more appreciated and have made more of a difference than you know. Kudos!

WRITERS...

Wait! Don't painstakingly copy every single URL in this list into your browser – visit kamerabooks.co.uk/resources and save on your desktop, so you can click/copy and paste and browse at your leisure. I will also try to make sure it's updated with anything interesting I find, or if any of the links here go dead.

WRITING, FILMMAKING & CAREER ADVICE WEBSITES

These websites, services, groups, pages and chats will help you get your screenplay written; answer your questions; and/or get your work 'out there'.

- **Bang2write:** www.bang2write.com Tips, How Tos and Q&As on screenwriting, creativity, filmmaking, social media, networking, inspiration and self-promotion.

- **Bang2writers:** Online Writers' Groups at: www.facebook.com/Bang2writers or search 'Bang2writers' at www.Linkedin.com in the groups section.

- **The B2W Required Reading List:** http://bitly.com/u/o_4h0h9gl8st A free e-library of links bundles on all things writing and filmmaking, including feature film investment and transmedia, as well as social media and submissions.

- **Twitter.** Twitter is not the 'time suck' you think… if you use it right! Check these out:

  #scriptchat. http://scriptchat.blogspot.co.uk There are usually two moderated chats every Sunday, Euro at 8pm GMT and 10pm GMT it's US chat. There are dedicated topics and guests each week, plus the #scriptchat hashtag is used throughout the week by writers seeking information, as well as sharing tips and links.

  #amwriting. Writers use this hashtag to share information and chat about what they're working on. Remember, the more people who know what you're writing and what you do, the more likely you will find collaborators and people who can take your work somewhere.

  #FF is Follow Friday and **#WW** stands for 'Writer Wednesday'. Check out the #FF and #WW posts and find out who is worth following. Engage them in conversation. What's the worst that can happen?

  #filmmaking, #GFilm, #londonSWF are hashtags where you can find people talking about actually making films, including producers.

  Other hashtags worth a look include #askagent, #subtip, #querytip, #writing, #screenwriting, #writetip, #writingtip, #scriptwriting, #rewrites, #scriptnotes, #screenplays, #screenwriters, #movies.

There are stacks more hashtags and new ones pop up all the time. Get on Twitter and find them – and find the people you seek!

- **LinkedIn.** There are lots of groups for writers on LinkedIn. My favourites include 'UK Screenwriters' and 'Screenwriters Network Worldwide' because they are always quite lively, with lots of discussions going on, but there are loads of others. Use the search facility to find them and connect with as many writing and filmmaking professionals as you can – but never spam people.

- **Facebook.** There are loads of great FB pages and groups dedicated to writing and discussion. The liveliest ones that pop up in my inbox the most are:

Guerilla Film Maker:
www.facebook.com/groups/guerillafilm/

Talent Circle Film Network:
www.facebook.com/groups/2457086898/

The Scriptwriter:
www.facebook.com/groups/139894528009/
Check out The Scriptwriter Dominic Carver on Twitter: @DomCarver.

Screenwriting U:
www.facebook.com/ScreenwritingU

New Writers Writing Screenplays:
www.facebook.com/groups/2212470452/

Good in a Room: (pitching advice)
www.facebook.com/GoodInARoom
Stephanie is also author of *Good in a Room*, available via Amazon. You can find her on Twitter as @goodinaroom.

But there are loads more. Just keep an eye out and 'like' everything. You never know where it might lead.

And, finally, these are my personal favourite free websites that offer articles and advice on screenwriting and your career:

- **Seth's blog:** www.sethgodin.com
Not strictly a screenwriting website, but most of what Seth says can be applied to being a professional writer. He offers succinct and to the point advice about managing your creative aspirations and your career. A must-read. Find Seth on Twitter: @ThisisSethsBlog.

- **Lee Jessup:** www.leejessup.com/home/
Lee is a Screenwriting Career Coach and offers no-nonsense advice on how to build your screenwriting career and get your work out there. Follow her on Twitter: @LeeZJessup.

- **Women & Hollywood:**
http://blogs.indiewire.com/womenandhollywood/
A great site that puts women at the forefront of screenwriting, movies and filmmaking; its founder Melissa Silverstein is a tireless campaigner. Follow her on Twitter: @melsil.

- **ScriptMag:** www.scriptmag.com, @scriptmag.
A great site on all things screenwriting, with alternative views of movies and writing from various contributors. Well worth a look and moderated by Jeanne Veillete Bowerman aka @jeannevb on Twitter.

- **Go Into The Story:**
www.gointothestory.blcklst.com and @GoIntoTheStory on Twitter. Run by screenwriter Scott Myers, who also runs 'The Quest' screen-writing course. GITs is the official site of The Black List (next).

- **The Black List/The Black Board:**
http://blcklst.com and @theblcklst on Twitter.
The best unproduced screenplays list, which has recently ventured into paid script listing. Take a look. Also, its sister site/forum, The Black Board, is at http://theblackboard.blcklst.com and @TheBlackBoard on Twitter.

- **Festival Formula:** www.festivalformula.com, @festivalformula
  Consultant Katie McCullough helps filmmakers with film festival strategy, submissions, crowdfunding and social media presence.

- **Script Secrets:**
  www.scriptsecrets.net from William Martell, @wcmartell on Twitter. Bill is the king of the cable movie and I've probably recommended his brilliant article '16 Steps To Better Scene Description' more than any other screenwriting article, ever.

- **John August:** www.johnaugust.com and @johnaugust on Twitter. Top screenwriter and director shares his screenwriting insights and answers writers' questions.

- **Wordplayer:** www.wordplayer.com
  Veteran screenwriters Ted Elliott and Terry Rossio offer their insights on screenwriting and working in Hollywood.

- **Sell Your Screenplay:**
  www.sellingyourscreenplay from Ashley Scott Meyers.
  A great website that breaks down how to get your work out there, Ashley Scott Meyers also has an 'email blast' service.

- **The International Screenwriters' Association:** http://networkisa.org
  A useful resource and monthly newsletter that offers lots of good advice to screenwriters on writing and pitching.

- **ReadWatchWrite:** http://readwatchwrite.com, also @RWWFilm and www.facebook.com/readwatchwrite
  You will have heard the screenwriting mantra 'read lots of scripts'. Brad has set the challenge of: read the script; watch the movie; reread the script – and see how your perception of the script/film changes. Well worth doing.

- **Scriptwriting In The UK:**
  www.dannystack.blogspot.co.uk, also @ScriptwritingUK on Twitter and www.facebook.com/ScriptwritingUK

Danny Stack is a screenwriter and filmmaker in his own right who also reads screenplays. His blog is a great UK-orientated screenwriting resource.

- **Projector Films:** www.projectorfilms.com
  Tim Clague is a BAFTA-nominated scriptwriter and filmmaker, offering up his alternative views on getting our work made/out there. Check out The Scriptwriter's Life here, a great visual on your work: http://scriptwriterslife.com

- **UK Scriptwriters – podcast:** Check out Danny Stack and Tim Clague talking screenwriting, here: https://itunes.apple.com/gb/podcast/uk-scriptwriters/id384710944 It's FREE.

- **On The Page Podcast:** Renowned script consultant Pilar Alessandra's (@onthepage) free podcast. Subscribe here: https://itunes.apple.com/gb/podcast/on-the-page-screenwriting/id262077408

Make sure you check out iTunes for more podcasts. There are lots dedicated to writing and filmmaking – and most of them free or costing pennies.

PEER REVIEW/ SCRIPT HOSTING AND PITCHING SITES

These websites offer writers the chance to host and/or pitch their work, either for free or for a fee. Make sure you check out all the T&Cs and/or guidelines before you get started (if applicable).

- **Zoetrope:** www.zoetrope.com, @Zoetrope_Mag.
  A 'virtual studio' for writers and filmmakers, set up in 2000. Membership is free.

- **Inktip:** www.inktip.com
  Possibly the most well-established, paid-for pitching platform; writers can buy listings on the website or in InkTip's magazine. Inktip boasts a pretty impressive number of productions of the scripts listed.

- **Amazon Studios:** www.studio.amazon.com, @Amazon_Studios. Quite a few writers have made it to development stage with this initiative so far, though at the time of writing none has been produced.

- **Shooting People:** www.shootingpeople.org, also @ShootingPeople on Twitter and www.facebook.com/shootingpeoples Subscription is £35 per year but gives screenwriters and filmmakers access to a number of bulletins, events and opportunities, including a weekly dedicated script pitch bulletin.

- **Mandy:** www.mandy.com, @mandyfilmtv. Another free comprehensive listings of jobs and various other opportunities.

- **Social Media.** Use social media for 'shout outs' on your own work or for peer review; don't be too aggressive or too timid and you're bound to find people. The best times to post are when the most people are online, which is typically 8.30am; 1pm; 5pm. There are also tools that run diagnostics of when your own followers are specifically online. Check out ones like Tweriod or sites like www.mashable.com / @mashable for more information on using your social media effectively.

- **Google!** That's right... don't wait for opportunities to land in your inbox, check out the internet every week at least for leads and/or set up Google alerts. Good search terms include (but are not limited to) 'script lead'; 'call for scripts'; 'unsolicited scripts welcome'; 'script call'; 'looking for screenplays'; 'searching for scripts', etc. In addition, Script Angel's Hayley McKenzie (@HayleyMckenzie1) has a BRILLIANT run down of UK production companies that accept unsolicited scripts, which you can find here:
http://scriptangel.wordpress.com/2013/01/17/production-companies-uk-accepting-unsolicited-scripts/

Whenever you find what looks like a good script lead and/or place to pitch, DO check the following:

- Have you heard of the person/place making the call?

- If you haven't, can you do a search on the company or person making the script call?

- Does the person have an IMDb listing or website or other online presence?

- Does the person or place making the script call respond to tweets or similar?

- Do you know anyone who has made a submission to this person or place? What was the outcome?

If in doubt, be sure to Google them and check whether they turn up on the Writer Beware! Blog, which you can find at www.writerbeware.com and http://accrispin.blogspot.co.uk

Remember: reputable agents and producers will NEVER ask you to pay for your own readers' reports or to pay them money to 'take your work to market'. So don't fall for this; it's a scam.

EVENTS, COURSES & TRAINING

There are so many events, it's impossible to list them all... so I've attempted to list those that are free or charge nominal fees or that offer the most exposure to writers in terms of networking and self-promotion, including pitching, as recommended by my Bang2writers and social network.

- **The Writers' Guild of Great Britain** frequently holds events for free or nominal fees, check out their website for details: www.writersguild.org.uk/news-a-features/events

- **The British Film Institute** and **BAFTA:** Check out the various courses, initiatives, schemes and events run by signing up for their newsletters at www.bfi.org.uk and www.bafta.org

- **The BBC Writersroom** runs free and low-cost events throughout the year, so keep an eye on their website for details. FYI, the Writersroom no longer accepts screenplays all year round, but instead offers 'windows' during which writers can submit work for consideration. Find out more details here:
  www.bbc.co.uk/writersroom/send-a-script/

- **Chris Jones:** www.chrisjonesblog.com and @livingspiritpix
  Chris's blog is a real shot in the arm for any writer who wants to know how films get made, from film financing up. You can take his Guerilla Filmmaker Masterclass www.guerillamasterclass.com, or his renowned 'Gone Fishing' course online www.gonefishingseminar.com

- **London Screenwriters' Festival:**
  www.londonscreenwritersfestival.com and www.facebook.com/londonswf. Held the last weekend of every October, LSF is the premier event for screenwriters and filmmakers, attracting a huge host of talented speakers and delegates, as well as big players, including Hollywood producers, in the speed-pitching event. LSF is the place to take your polished projects and make serious inroads to your career.

- **London Breakfast Club:** www.facebook.com/londonbreakfastclub
  Held throughout the year, roughly £16 per event: a great speaker and a great breakfast... plus networking!

- **Women In Film And Television (WFTV):** www.wftv.org.uk
  Check out the initiatives and interests of this influential organisation, run by CEO Kate Kinninmont (@WomenInFilmKate).

- **The Great American Pitchfest:**
  https://pitchfest.com, @thepitchfest and www.facebook.com/GAPFGreatAmericanPitchfest. GAPF takes place in June each year in Hollywood and its founders, Signe Olynyk (@Screenwriter12) and Bob Schultz (@pitchfestbob) ran the Pitchfest for @LondonSWF.

- **Hollywood Field Trip:** www.hollywoodfieldtrip.com
  Run by Guerilla Filmmaker's Genevieve Jolliffe, HFT takes a small group of delegates out to Hollywood to meet agents, managers and producers and boasts an impressive success rate, so check it out. A must for any British screenwriter wanting to crack LA.

- **Raindance:** www.raindance.org or @Raindance
  Offers great tips and articles for writers and filmmakers about the realities of screenwriting and filmmaking. The Raindance Film Festival happens every year, plus Elliot Grove has written books and other training about film production. Make sure you subscribe to his site.

- **Power to The Pixel:** http://powertothepixel.com
  Dedicated film and cross-platform/transmedia event, usually running in October of each year. A great event for writers to keep their finger on the pulse of changing tech/ways of delivering content, plus producers and agents can be found here, so networking opportunities are good.

- **BVE:** http://www.bvexpo.com
  Billed as the 'essential broadcast and production technology event', knowing as much as you can about the changing face of tech in film is again a great idea, especially as many producers will also be present.

- **The Underwire Film Festival:** www.underwirefilmfestival.com
  A dedicated celebration of female filmmakers, Underwire is not a 'closed shop' to men and is a lovely, inclusive environment.

- **The Stellar Network:**
  http://stellarnetwork.com and @StellarNetwork.
  A research and development agency that works with emerging talent, Stellar Network invites submissions from writers for its dedicated pitching sessions at BAFTA. Subscribe for info on these calls.

- **The BAFTA Rocliffe New Writing Forum:**
  www.rocliffe.com, also @rocliffeforum.
  Initiative connecting emerging writers with new filmmaking talent.

- **Euroscript:** www.euroscript.co.uk
  also @Euroscript and www.facebook.com/Euroscript Euroscript
  offers script reports and training/mentorship for writers and runs
  evening courses.

- **Southern Script Festival:**
  www.facebook.com/groups/140419319345469/
  Held at Bournemouth University in beautiful Dorset, SSF started
  in 2011 and is held by BU students for new writers.

- **Other film festivals:**
  Film festivals are great places to meet producers, agents and
  filmmakers. There are so many film festivals, both in the UK and
  worldwide, that it's impossible to list them here. So check out
  this directory for a film festival near you, provided by the British
  Council: http://film.britishcouncil.org/festivals-directory

BOOKS

*There are so many books dedicated to writing, it can be hard to know
which ones to go for. I have compiled a Pinterest board of the books
most recommended by my Bang2writers. Find it here:*
http://pinterest.com/bang2write/bang2write-books/

The books I recommend Bang2writers read most:

- *Writing Drama* by Yves Lavandier
- *Screenplay* by Syd Field
- *The 21st Century Screenwriter* by Linda Aronson
- *Aristotle's Poetics For Screenwriters* by Michael Tiernan
- *Teach Yourself Screenwriting* by Raymond Frensham
- *Successful Models For Filmmakers* by John Sweeney

SCREENWRITING COMPETITIONS

Here are the 'big six' feature screenplay contests. Most of these sites also offer articles, information and tips on screenwriting. Bang2writers have won and placed highly in all these contests, many of them with thrillers:

- **The Nicholl Fellowship:** www.oscars.org/awards/nicholl/
- **Bluecat:** www.bluecatscreenplay.com, @BluecatPictures and www.facebook.com/groups/BlueCatScreenwriting/
- **Final Draft Big Break:** www.finaldraft.com/products/big-break/
- **Screenwriting Goldmine:** http://awards.screenwritinggoldmine.com
- **Just Effin Entertain Me:** www.justeffing.com/screenwriting-competition/ 2013-competition/open/ and @Julie_Gray
- **Scriptapolooza:** http://scriptapolooza.com
- **The PAGE Awards:** http://pageawards.com. @PAGEawards and www.facebook.com/pageawards

You will notice that, barring Screenwriting Goldmine, there is a strong US bias for feature screenplay contests. There are, of course, many, many other screenwriting contests. **Check out the Movie Bytes Screenwriting Competitions Directory**, which handily categorises all contests, including by genre: www.moviebytes.com/directory.cfm.

SCRIPT READERS & SCRIPT EDITORS

There are many, many readers online to choose from, but these are the only readers Bang2write officially recommends and/or refers 'Bang2writers' to when they want a second opinion, or I am too busy. They range in price from moderately expensive to cheap; I don't believe in paying several hundred pounds for feedback, but I also believe 'pay peanuts, you get monkeys'!

- **Michelle Goode**, So Fluid Script Consultancy, @SoFluid, www.writesofluid.com (www.facebook.com/writesofluid)

- **Hayley McKenzie**, Script Angel, @HayleyMckenzie1, www.scriptangel.co.uk (www.facebook.com/scriptangel)

- **Yvonne Grace**, Script Advice Writers' Room, @YVONNEGRACE1, www.scriptadvice.co.uk (www.facebook.com/groups/237330119115/)

- **Andy Wooding**, Film Doctor, @Film_Doctor, http://filmdoctor.wordpress.com (www.facebook.com/FilmGP)

- **Samuel Hutchinson**, Hutch Scripts, @SamHutchi, http://hutchscripts.wordpress.com

- **Richard Cosgrove**, Camden Script Analysis (@rcosgrove), https://camdenscriptanalysis.wordpress.com

- **Ellin Stein**, Solid Script Services, @ellinst, www.solidscripts.co.uk

- **Scott 'The Reader' Mullen**, http://sixtybucknotes.blogspot.co.uk

- **Mark Sanderson**, My Blank Page, @scriptcat, http://scriptcat.wordpress.com

When thinking about employing a paid-for reader for the first time, make sure you check out their websites and social media profiles. Also, ask the readers for testimonials or your own colleagues for their recommendations.

OTHER

- **Crowdfunding platforms:** Kickstarter and IndieGoGo are possibly the most well known, but there are many, many others. This directory is a handy list: http://coolintl.com/comprehensive-directory-of-crowdfunding-platforms/

- **Professional sites:** knowing who is making what, with whom, and by what date gives you more information for your own projects and more credibility as an industry professional. Consider upgrading your free accounts and taking out the following subscriptions:

Done Deal Pro: www.donedealpro.com/default.aspx
IMDB Pro: https://secure.imdb.com/signup/index.html
Moviescope: www.moviescopemag.com
Screen International: www.screendaily.com
Sight & Sound: www.bfi.org.uk/taxonomy/term/467
The Scoggins Report: http://scogginsreport.com

INDEX

A

Abuse 9, 20, 43, 51, 61, 72, 113,
    120, 123, 127, 128
Actors 14, 34, 55, 63, 68-67, 107,
    122, 129, 163, 165
Adaptation 15-19, 47, 60, 75-76, 129
Age 17, 18-19, 181
Animals 55, 78, 159
Archetype 117
Audience 10, 13, 14, 17-18, 23-26,
    28, 30-34, 36, 38, 42-45, 50,
    53-54, 57-59, 69, 72-73, 84-86,
    88-93, 95, 97-98, 103-104,
    107, 117, 119, 120, 128, 131,
    134, 135-137, 139, 140-143,
    145, 147, 149-150, 152, 155,
    163, 166-167, 173, 177, 181-
    182, 185, 187
Awards 19, 30-31, 41, 42, 75, 201

B

Beautiful Thing 20, 62, 120-129
Behaviour 167, 168
Believable 29, 105
Best Picture 90, 92, 140
Biopic 15-17, 48, 91-92, 144, 149
Blue Valentine 23-24, 26-27, 131-
    139, 146, 186

C

Cancer Hair 19, 31-41, 163, 187
Case study 23, 31, 38, 46, 47, 61,
    79, 99, 120, 150, 171
Change agent 94, 118, 140-142,
    145, 148-149
Characterisation 56, 117, 119,
    124, 133, 141, 142, 147, 162,
    163
Children 41, 50, 52, 62, 76, 78,
    96, 103, 114, 124, 132-133,
    159, 175, 176-177, 186
Cianfrance, Derek 26-27, 186
Clarke, Noel 79-82, 128
Cliché 21, 22, 29, 72, 77, 88-89,
    139, 179, 186, 188
Closed protagonist 141, 142, 145,
    149, 150
Concept 14, 24, 58, 77, 93, 109,
    118-119, 131, 145, 163, 176
Conflict 44, 46, 56-70, 88, 97, 116,
    119, 127, 135, 138, 146, 169,
    174, 185, 187
Controversy 86
Copyright 47, 49, 55, 75, 76, 77,
    78, 122
Critics 30, 92, 163

D

Dallas Buyers Club 27, 189
Dear Frankie 19, 41, 43, 61-70, 186
Depressing 19, 21, 44, 72, 89, 97,
    98, 127, 128, 136, 154, 179,
    185, 187
Dialogue 39, 59, 150, 154, 161,
    163, 165-167, 169, 170
Director 17, 18, 19, 23, 39, 40-41,
    59, 62, 64, 101, 156, 171, 185
Disney 19, 47-55, 154, 171, 173,
    174-175, 177, 186
Distribution 34, 40, 41, 77, 175, 186
Domestic 72, 110, 127, 128
Drama 13-15, 19, 21, 22, 28-31, 42-
    44, 59-61, 72-74, 88-99, 109-120
Dramatic context 145, 146, 158
Dramedy 187

E

Elwes, Cassian 27, 189
Emotional truth 44-46, 54, 85, 179,
    181
Episodic 144, 146, 148-149

F

Fatherhood 151, 162
Female 18, 19, 32, 37, 41, 47, 50,
    53, 64, 69, 73, 93, 96, 113,
    114-116, 173, 174, 199
Film festivals 34, 40-41, 42, 75, 200
Filmmaker 18, 21-26, 28-31, 32,
    34, 38, 39, 41, 43, 45, 71-72,
    77, 82, 86, 92, 106-109, 118,
    128, 131, 147, 159, 160, 175,
    188, 195-196, 198-200
Flashback 49, 54, 113, 135, 143,
    147, 157, 162
Funding 40-41, 43, 122, 202

G

Gender 18-19, 41, 53, 64, 73, 88
Genre 11, 13-14, 18, 23, 24-26,
    28-31, 34, 43, 56-59, 73, 88,
    90, 96, 108, 120, 129, 130-
    131, 136, 138-139, 162-163,
    165, 170, 178, 189, 201
Gibb, Andrea 41, 61-70
Glass ceiling 81
Goals 39, 40, 145, 168, 182
Gosling, Ryan 23, 24, 26, 131, 186

H

Hackston, Gail 31, 128, 187
Harvey, Jonathan 120
Heisserer, Eric 38, 150-153, 156-
    162, 185, 189
Henry, Linda 122
Hero 47, 49, 73, 93, 111, 124,
    144, 151
High concept 14, 24, 58, 138
Hollywood 25-27, 31, 43, 47, 48,
    133, 151, 152, 175, 185, 193-
    194, 198, 199
Hours 20, 38, 150-164, 189

I

IMDb 13, 15-18, 31, 42, 180, 197,
    203
Internal 37, 44, 46, 56-58, 88, 96,
    119, 135, 138, 169, 185, 187
Investment 27, 39, 76-77, 175, 191

J

Jones, Chris 108, 171-177, 198

K

Kerr, Clare 99, 102, 107
Kidulthood 20, 79-87, 129

L

Loglines 19, 136-139
Low-budget 10, 22, 25, 42, 78,
    100, 102, 120, 129

M

Marcel, Kelly 47-53, 55, 148, 175,
    185
Mead, Adrian 99-108, 159
Message 10, 37, 47,58-60, 71-74,
    80, 82-83, 85, 91, 97, 106,
    115, 119, 131, 136, 140, 144,
    149, 173-174, 177, 181, 186
Morality 20, 59, 72, 79, 84, 86
Mother/Mum 19, 22, 72, 41, 50-52,
    62-63, 66-68, 84, 88, 92, 103,
    104, 109, 114-115, 124-127,
    131, 135, 144, 151, 155, 186

N

Night People 20, 99-108, 122, 129,
    159, 186
Non-linear 44, 47, 49, 54, 73, 94,
    132, 137-138, 143, 145-149,
    150, 182, 186

O

Opportunities 21, 29, 37, 41, 45, 68-
    69, 81, 107, 119, 129, 142, 164,
    168, 177, 183-184, 196, 199
Owen, Alison 47-49, 175

P

Pain 46, 53, 167, 189
Parent 43, 60, 63, 74, 96, 109,
    114, 116, 126, 151, 176-177
Passion 178
Performance 151, 152, 159, 160,
    162

Personal 13-14, 18, 20, 24, 36, 43,
    44, 46, 57, 95, 97, 138, 151,
    155, 162
Pitch 22, 28, 74, 77-78, 109, 137-
    138, 185, 192, 194-199
Plot 35, 56, 64, 69, 83, 94-95,
    131, 133, 143, 145, 147-150,
    163, 165, 182
Portfolio 28
Portmanteau 20, 99-100, 104,
    106-108, 183, 186
Production 13-14, 29, 32, 63, 99,
    101-102, 106, 122, 160, 163-
    164, 178, 196, 199

R

Race 18-19,80, 88, 103, 115
Representation 80, 84
Research 18-19, 34, 38, 63, 68-69,
    75, 76, 85, 92, 128, 163, 169,
    178, 199
Rocketboy 20, 171-178, 186
Ruby Films 48, 53, 55

S

Sample 29-30, 106-107, 188
Saving Mr Banks 19, 43, 47-55,
    129, 148, 166, 175, 186
Script development 68
Short Film 10, 19, 21, 31-41, 42,
    62-63, 69, 100, 106-108, 186
Social Media 34, 68, 114, 165,
    180, 191, 194, 196, 202
Stereotype 78, 117-118, 128
Structure 10, 30, 49, 54, 79, 82,
    86, 94, 131, 142-149, 181-182
Struggle 19, 44, 46, 57, 97, 131,
    151, 162, 187
Suicide 9, 20, 79, 82-83, 103, 113-114

T

Theme 10, 47, 58-61, 71-74, 79,
    86, 95-96, 100, 106-107, 108,
    119, 136, 142, 144, 149, 173,
    181, 187
Transformative arc 33, 120, 133-
    136, 140-142, 145-147

V

Violence 9, 20, 80-83, 110-111,
    114-115
Visuals 37, 39, 167, 169-170

W

Walker, Paul 151-153, 158-160,
    163, 189
War 29, 43, 61, 90, 144
Williams, Michelle 23, 24, 26, 131,
    186
Woman-centric 63, 96
Write What You Know 38, 101, 169

About Us

In addition to Creative Essentials, Oldcastle Books has a number of other imprints, including No Exit Press, Kamera Books, Pulp! The Classics, Pocket Essentials and High Stakes Publishing **> oldcastlebooks.co.uk**

Checkout the kamera film salon for independent, arthouse and world cinema **> kamera.co.uk**

For more information, media enquiries and review copies please contact **> marketing@oldcastlebooks.com**